AUDITIONING IN THE 21ST CENTURY

AUDITIONING IN THE 21ST CENTURY

An essential handbook for those auditioning and working in the German-speaking theater 'fest' system.

William A. Killmeier and Nada Radakovich

Writers Club Press
San Jose New York Lincoln Shanghai

Auditioning in the 21st Century
An essential handbook for those auditioning
and working in the German-speaking theater 'fest' system.

Writers Club Press
an imprint of iUniverse.com, Inc.

For information address:
iUniverse.com, Inc.
5220 S 16th, Ste. 200
Lincoln, NE 68512
www.iuniverse.com

ISBN: 0-595-18668-8

Printed in the United States of America

Contents

Foreword

Oh, to be an opera singer! It sounds so romantic, and in many ways it is. Nothing can be more rewarding than sharing one's talents and abilities with the general public through this classic singing/acting medium. As those of you who have purchased this book already know by now, this opera "business" is much more than the art of singing and acting. The following pages present a view shared by two singers who are "out there" making a living performing.

We are Americans who have lived in Germany and have steadily worked in many opera houses there since the 1991/1992 season. We are having satisfying but very different careers.

Ms. Radakovich sang as a *fest**-employed lyric coloratura soprano for four seasons and now freelances at various theaters and festivals. In addition, she sings with operetta tours as well as concert and oratorio engagements.

Mr. Killmeier has worked as a *fest Kavalierbariton* in three different theaters, and has guested in others as well. Since the 1991/1992 season he has performed over 50 different roles in nearly every baritone *Fach** (shattering the myth of the "unshakable" German *Fachsystem*).

Just because the timbre of our two voices varies, our perspectives on this profession do not. Much, if not most, of the information contained in this handbook is indisputable. We acknowledge that many readers may or may not agree with some of our ideas and/or opinions; nevertheless, we offer this information with humility and sincerity.

We have collected information from numerous singers, stage directors, conductors, agents, administrators, as well as our own personal experience. Some of these individuals are German, and some are not. Some have *only* been *fest*, and some have *never* been *fest*; all of our sources, however, are working, income-producing professionals.

This book was written with the hope that your auditioning experience in Germany (or in the other German-speaking countries) will go much more smoothly than ours did nearly ten years ago. We also would like this handbook to function as an all-inclusive guide, enabling you to be concerned exclusively with the business of singing.

We wish our colleagues the greatest success and happiness while following their dreams by pursuing what they love the most and do the best. Good luck!

*For purposes of this book, *fest* refers to a salaried position in any theater throughout the German-speaking countries. The German dictionary defines *Fach* as a "compartment" or "field" (of work). In the singing business, *Fach* refers to the voice type. The plural for *Fach* is *Fächer*.

Preface

The authors have put together a compendium of information for the young American wanting to sing and audition in Germany, Austria, and Switzerland. They are to be congratulated for their successful efforts. Through the detailed study of this handbook, the neophyte will have it much easier in these countries, with regard to auditioning for agents and for the general auditions theaters call. Their traveling will be much facilitated through the vast amount of information given in detail about the rail system, especially in Germany. A particular service has been rendered by these young author-singers in their explanation of the bureaucracy of "red-tape" pertaining to visas, living, and working permits, and to the completely foreign experience for an American of registering with the police. Bravo to Nada Radakovich and William Killmeier who know from personal experience of what they are writing.

George Fortune, Baritone
Deutsche Oper Berlin
Metropolitan Opera

Acknowledgments

We would like to thank the following artists and friends who gave so generously of their time and thoughts: Karen Stone, Granville Walker, Ursula Fortune, *Kammersänger* George Fortune, *Kammersänger* Dietrich Fischer-Diskau, *Kammersängerin* Marianne Fischer-Kupfer, *Kammersänger* Andreas Becker, Brian Nedvin, Martina Borgstedt, Stephan and Vineeta Kohorst, Sharon Cogburn, Larry Minth, Niel Rishoi, Daniel Gundlach, and especially Sallie Satterthwaite for her honest and direct editorial suggestions and changes.

Introduction

Nada Radakovich and William Killmeier have put together an amazingly thorough, absolutely indispensable book of information for the opera singer wishing to audition in Germany. With this book in hand, prospective artists will be guided expertly through the various aspects of living and auditioning as a singer, in a country where matters function in a way all its own. No vital facts are omitted, nothing is left to chance; every avenue of living, traveling, shopping, lodging, eating, communicating—you name it—is explored, covered, expanded upon and clarified with refreshing candor and forthright simplicity. Furthermore, these writers hold forth with sharp observations and well-based advice, with the unerring sagacity of those who have lived and learned through audition processes—the hard way. With the information presented in these pages, much trouble and even grief will be safely eliminated. No singer should even *enter* Germany without this priceless book.

Niel Rishoi
Author, *Edita Gruberova: Ein Portrait (1996 Atlantis Musikbuch)*

PART ONE

Preparing For Your Audition Tour

"*Most of the time just great singing isn't all you need! Besides comfortable shoes, lots of safety pins, and nerves of steel, your 'presentation' is just as important. I won a competition once, and when talking to the judges afterwards, one told me that they knew I was the winner even before I opened my mouth just by the way I walked onto the stage. You need confidence. This comes by realizing they WANT you to be good. They are on your side, so go in there and give them what they want! 'Present' yourself as if their long drought is over and you are what they've been looking for all along. They just may believe it!*"

Jennifer Larmore, Mezzo Soprano
Metropolitan Opera

Chapter One

This Ever-Changing Business

There have been major changes in the German *Festsystem* during the past ten years. Those of us who went to college in the late seventies and early eighties were often given the impression that there were endless singing opportunities awaiting us in the German-speaking countries. Whether that was ever true or not will always be argued. Nevertheless, ever since the Iron Curtain fell, no one can dispute the dramatic increase in competition throughout the opera industry.

When Nada got her first *fest* contract, she was one of five American soloists in her theater. There were a total of twelve *fest* soloists, and of those, only four were German. Where William is presently engaged, there are 25 *fest* soloists. Only four of them are Americans. Thirteen of the singers are German.

The falling of the Berlin Wall ten years ago did provide new opportunities for many American singers in the former East Germany. However, for the first time since the wall was built, it also provided the chance for those from the East to move west and seek out jobs for themselves. We are not only referring to those from the eastern European countries, but also those from the Far East. Out of the twenty men in William's opera chorus, four of them are Koreans. We assume that means the word has finally spread around the world, "If you want to make a living singing, go to Germany!"

Several years ago, I (William) was invited to speak at a seminar held on "The Singing Voice" at the Charité Hospital in Berlin. I was asked by Dr. Jürgen Wendler and Dr. Wolfram Seidner, authors of *Die Sänger Stimme (The Singer's Voice)*, to address the reason so many American singers were working in Germany. Boy, did I have to be careful! I couldn't just say, "Because Americans are superior singers!" Many believe that that has been the unspoken attitude of most Americans for several years, but it's not that simple, nor true, for that matter.

This is basically how I answered the doctors' question:

"The reason for so many American singers living in Germany may be partly due to the pioneering spirit that still exists today in America, the drive to follow the 'American dream.' The fact is, one really does have the freedom to do whatever he or she wishes in the States. Yes, a singer may have limited financial resources, but even that can be remedied if he or she is willing to wait enough tables, paint enough houses, or learn word processing.

"In Germany, you cannot simply walk down the street to a construction sight, and ask the foreman for a job. Nor is it so easy finding a part-time job waiting tables or doing word processing. In fact, it's almost impossible. One must have a work permit to perform these jobs. Every job also seems to require a special *Ausbildung* (education or training). Even after that is over, there is often an internship or probation period. It is not difficult to see how quickly one would get discouraged as a native German singer, that is *if* they had an American singer's mentality (that of being willing to do almost anything to reach one's dreams, even if it means cleaning toilets every now and then to pay the bills). I don't know of one working American singer who has not, at one time or another during their adult life, done something they really would have preferred not doing, just so they could pay the bills. In Germany, things are not that simple."

Another obvious difference I pointed out in my speech (and I personally believe this is the main difference) is that *Germans do not pay a dime to go to college.* Yes, of course, the German public does, through taxes, and how! However, the student does not. In fact, they even get an allowance to go. (Would you believe that recently throughout Germany, students were actually *on strike* because they felt they were not being given enough teachers? Try to figure that one out.) The majority of German college students do not complete their studies until they are almost 26 years old. I actually know some who are past 30 and still in college. Obviously, there is no motivation to "move on" if your tuition is being paid by someone else, as well as some of your living expenses.

I don't know about you, but nearly fifteen years ago, I was paying more than $10,000 a year to go to a decent music school. I somehow managed with the help of family members, various financial aid, and student loans. When I graduated I had $15,000 of outstanding student loans. I don't have to tell you, that after having paid for most of my education myself, and bearing that kind of debt when I graduated, I was *very* motivated to "move on" and was definitely more driven than I otherwise would have been.

I gave that speech several years ago. Since that time, things have changed significantly. This will shock many people, but the fact is, *Americans no longer dominate the opera singing industry in the German-speaking theaters.* Some of you may have a hard time accepting this, but the statistics do not lie. We could talk *ad nauseum* about why this is so, but the outstanding reason is that *there is a new generation of well-trained German singers.* This is clearly the result of an abundance of excellent voice teachers and coaches, German as well as non-German, who are living and teaching in Germany, Switzerland, and Austria. It only makes common sense. When fewer singing and conducting jobs exist, more and more singers/coaches/conductors are driven out of performing, and into the teaching and coaching profession or, for that matter, into other professions altogether. Why do you think there is an endless supply of excellent teachers and coaches in the States? We believe the answer is obvious. There simply are not enough performing opportunities to go around for the number of capable artists who long to perform.

The tremendous budget cutbacks in the theater system are another reason for the reduction in singing jobs in Germany. Our own theater's budget is 30 percent less than it was five years ago. Many theaters have merged with others or closed entirely. Others have had to let go of the ballet, while some have actually let go of the entire orchestra. So it just makes sense to assume that eventually a certain number of singing jobs will be jeopardized as well.

Having said all that, we *still* maintain that *nothing beats singing in the German fest system.* The amount of performing opportunities in the States can never be compared to those that exist in Germany. There will *always* be opportunities there for non-German singers, but they may not be as abundant as they once were. The amount of money poured into culture in Germany really is inconceivable to Americans. It was published in a major newspaper in 1994 that the cultural budget for the state of New York (*all* culture, *all* museums, ballet, music, etc.) was $55 million, and that it would soon be *cut in half.* During that same year, the *Deutsche Oper Berlin*'s budget *alone* was 120 million DM, about $80 million at the time. Think about that. And there are nearly 100 opera houses throughout Germany, Austria, and Switzerland—all with *fest* ensembles.

So, if you are looking for a place to sing full-time, a place to learn foreign languages, and perform an unlimited amount of repertoire, Germany is still the place to be. To give you an idea of just how many *full-time* employees there are in the German-speaking theaters, we have included the following statistics.

***

Full-Time Employees working in the German-Speaking Theaters	Men	Women	Total
Theater Administrative Directors	423	91	514
Costume & Set Designers	550	416	966
Conductors/Coaches/Accompanists	665	94	759
Ballet Instructors/Choreographers	148	98	246
Singers (Soloists)	1,528	1,050	2,578
Chorus Singers	1,628	1,675	3,303
Dancers	681	889	1,570
Stage Directors	518	133	651
Assistant Stage Directors	198	177	375
Prompters	78	282	36

Note: A more detailed list can be found in the *Deutsches Bühnen Jahrbuch.*

"A strong command of the German language will not only ensure your credibility on a professional level, but also provides the necessary and much appreciated social ease when dealing with theater colleagues and German locals."

Karen Stone
Souffleusse, Aalto-Theater Essen

Chapter Two

Language Skills

We cannot impress upon you too much the importance of your knowledge of the German language in today's market, written as well as spoken. It is our opinion that the days of singers going to Germany with no language skills (we will try to refrain from any tenor jokes here…) and landing a job are soon, if not already, over.

Consider the following scenario:

You have a country, specifically Germany, with 14.5 percent unemployment, as of this writing. The *Zentrale Bühnen-, Fernseh- und Filmvermittlung* (Central Stage, Television and Film Agency), commonly known as *ZBF*, is a branch of the *Arbeitsamt* (the Department of Labor) whose responsibility it is to find jobs for unemployed artists. Let's imagine for a moment that there is a specific theater looking for a Papageno in *The Magic Flute*, which has lots of spoken text. There are just as many German baritones on the agent's list as American—we will touch upon this later. To whom do you think *ZBF* is going to give preference when deciding whom to send to the audition? That's an easy one.

Try this one:

We have a friend who has sung *Königin der Nacht* (Queen of the Night in *The Magic Flute*) in probably five different theaters in Germany. She has received nothing but excellent reviews of her premières of the role, not only for her singing, but her flawless dialogue as well. When she recently sang for an agent (specifically for *Königin*), the agent told her, "There is no questioning your ability to do this role.

9

However, why should I send you to audition for 'Queen' when I have six other native-speaking Germans who do it just as well?"

Are you starting to get the point?

We are not trying to scare you here, but we want to drive home the importance of your getting a handle on this language *before* purchasing your plane ticket. Think about it. You've spent all these years honing your craft. You probably already spend at least $500 a month on voice lessons and coaching. *Doesn't it make common sense for you to spend some of that time and money on language lessons as well?*

Though the study of the German language is beyond the scope of this book, we have provided some examples of resumés, and audition letters, not only for soloists, but for chorus singers and accompanists as well. We would like to thank those colleagues, presently in the *fest* system, who provided actual resumés for us to reprint.

We strongly recommend William Owen's book *Towards A Career in Europe* for his Appendix B, which contains a superb list of German phrases, musical terms, and sample letters. In addition, in goes without saying that you should have a *Langenscheidts Taschenwörterbuch* (Langenscheidt's Pocket Dictionary) with you at all times.

***

William Killmeier, Baritone
(address, telephone, etc..)
xxxxxxxxxxxxxxx
xxxxxxxxxxxxxxxxxxx
xxxxxxxxxxxxxxx

EDUCATION: University of Georgia, Athens, Georgia
Westminster Choir College, Princeton, NJ

TEACHERS/COACHES: George Fortune (Deutsche Oper, Berlin)
John Fiorito (Metropolitan Opera, New York)
Don Wiggins
Judith Nicosia-Civitano
Dalton Baldwin
Glen Parker

AWARDS: Shoshana Foundation's William F. Gold Career Grant

SPECIAL NOTICES: After graduation from Westminster Choir College, William Killmeier became soloist and a member of The United States Army Band and The Army Chorus (Pershing's Own) in Washington, D.C. During his enlistment with the U.S. Army, Mr. Killmeier performed regularly for then-Vice President George Bush as well as George Schultz at the State Department, Caspar Weinberger and the Joint Chiefs of Staff.

THEATERS: Dortmund Stadttheater, fest from April1, 1996
Städtebundtheater Hof, fest 1995-1996
Landestheater Mecklenburg, Neustrelitz, fest 1992-1995
Aachener Theater, as guest
Staatstheater Kassel, as guest
Dessau Landestheater, as guest
Göttingen Syphoniker, as guest
Neubrandenburg Philharmonic, as guest
Spoleto Festival dei due Mondi, USA and Spoleto Italy
Washington Opera
Summer Opera Theater, Washington, D.C.

Opera Theater of Northern Virginia
Atlanta Opera
Bermuda Music Festival

***

William Killmeier, Baritone
(address, telephone, etc..)
xxxxxxxxxxxxxxx
xxxxxxxxxxxxxxxxxxxx
xxxxxxxxxxxxxxxx

AUSBILDUNG: University of Georgia, USA
                 Westminster Choir College, Princeton,NJ, USA

LEHRER: George Fortune (Deutsche Oper, Berlin, Metropolitan Opera,
                 New York)
                 John Fiorito (Metropolitan Opera, New York)
                 Don Wiggins
                 Judith Nicosia-Civitano
                 Dalton Baldwin
                 Glen Parker

STIPENDIUM: Shoshana Foundation's William F. Gold Career Grant

BESONDERE BEMERKUNGEN: Nach dem Abschluß des Westminster Choir Colleges ist William Killmeier Hauptsolist für die United States Army Band und den United States Army Chorus (Pershing's Own) in Washington, D.C. geworden. Während seiner Einstellung in der U.S. Armee hatte Herr Killmeier Gelegenheit, im Hause des damaligen Vizepräsidenten, George Bush, im Capitol, beim Außenministerium für Staatssekretär Schultz sowie Caspar Weinberger und den Generalstab zu singen.

THEATER: Dortmund Stadttheater, fest von 1. April 1996
                 Staatstheater Kassel, a.G.
                 Theater Aachen, a.G.
                 Städtebundtheater Hof, fest 1995-1996
                 Landestheater Mecklenburg, Neustrelitz, fest 1992-1995
                 Dessau Landestheater, a. G.
                 Göttingen Syphoniker, a. G.
                 Neubrandenburg Philharmonic, a. G.
                 Spoleto Festival dei due Mondi, USA u. Spoleto Italia
                 Washington Opera
                 Summer Opera Theater, Washington, D.C.
                 Opera Theater of Northern Virginia
                 Atlanta Opera
                 Burmuda Music Festival

***

ROLLEN:			
	Berlioz	*Les Troyens*	Chorèbe
	Bloch, Ernest	*Macbeth*	Macbeth
	Catalani	*La Wally*	Gellner
	Chausson	*Le Roi Arthus*	Arthus
		(Deutsche Erstaufführung)	
	Glass, Philip	*La Belle et la Bète*	La Bète
		(Deutsche Erstaufführung)	und Avenant
	Goldmark, Carl	*Königin von Saba*	Solomon
	Humperdink	*Hänsel und Gretel*	Peter
	Leoncavallo	*Pagliacci*	Sylvio
	Lortzing	*Zar u. Zimmermann*	Peter
	Mozart	*Figaros Hochzeit*	Il Conte
		Figaros Hochzeit	Figaro
		Die Zauberflöte	Papageno
		Don Giovanni	Don Giovanni
	Nicolai	*Lustige Weiber*	Fluth
	Pfitzner	*Der Arme Heinrich*	Dietrich
	Puccini	*Madame Butterfly*	Sharpless
		La Bohème	Marcello
		La Bohème	Schaunard
	Rihm, Wolfgang	*Jakob Lenz*	Jakob Lenz
	Rosenfeld, Gerhard	*Kniefall in Warschau*	Willy Brandt
		(Weltaufführung)	
	Rossini	*La Cenerentola (auf deutsch)*	Dandini
	Tchaikowsky	*Eugen Onegin (auf deutsch)*	Onegin
	Turnage, Mark Anthony	*The Silver Tassie*	Harry
	Verdi	*Aida*	Amonasro
		Don Carlos	Posa
		Falstaff	Ford
		La Forza del destino	Don Carlos
		Rigoletto	Rigoletto
		Il Trovatore	Di Luna
	Wagner	*Parsifal*	Amfortas
		Tannhäuser	Wolfram
	Weber	*Der Freischütz*	Ottokar

***

*** *Charlotte O'Hara, Mezzo Soprano* * * *
(address, telephone, etc..)

Professional Experience

Charlotte ~ *Werther*, San Francisco Lyric Opera, 1998.

Zerlina ~ *Don Giovanni*, Berkeley Opera, 1999.

Giulietta ~ *King for a Day*, by Verdi. Pocket Opera, San Francisco, 1999.

Secretary ~ *The Consul*, by Menotti, West Bay Opera, Palo Alto, 1999.

Nicklausse ~ *Tales of Hoffmann*, Pocket Opera, San Francisco, 1997-8.

Nancy ~ *Martha*, Pocket Opera, San Francisco, 1998.

Polinesso ~ *Ariodante*, concert format, Pocket Opera, San Francisco, 1997.

Judith ~ *Wuornos,* a new opera by Carla Lucero, Brava-Women in the Arts, San Francisco, 1998.

Mary Eastin ~ *The Dreamers*, by David Conte and Phillip Littel, World Premiere. Sonoma City Opera, 1996.

Second Lady ~ *The Magic Flute*, Berkely Opera, George Cleve, con., 1996.

Amoroso ~ *The Bridge of Sighs*, by Offenbach, Pocket Opera, San Francisco, 1995

Carmen ~ *Carmen*, San Francisco Opera Guild outreach program, 1996-97

Alice in Operaland, Holiday show, outreach program, Pocket Opera, 1996-8

Oratorio Solo Experience

~*Midnight Mass*, by Charpentier, Lakeside Presbyterian Church, San Francisco, 1998.

~*Coronation Mass*, by Mozart, Stanford Memorial Church, Palo Alto, 1998.

~*The Messiah*, abbreviated version, Concord, 1996.

~*Missa Brevis* in D Major, K. 194, by Mozart, Oberlin College Choir Tour, 1992.

~*Litanae Lauretanae*, K. 195, by Mozart, Oberlin College Choir, 1991.

Recitals

~Glimmerglass Young American Artist Program Recital Series, Cooperstown, NY, 1997.

~Noe Valley Concert Series, Noe Valley Ministry, San Francisco, 1996.

Awards and Honors

~Regional Finalist, Metropolitan Opera National Council Auditions, 1995.

~1st Place, Santa Clara University Art Song Festival Competition, 1994.

~National Finalist, National Society of Arts and Letters (NSAL) Competition, 1997.

~Prizewinner, East Bay Opera League, Oakland, CA, 1999.

Music Programs
~Glimmerglass Opera Young American Artist Program, Cooperstown, NY.
~American Institute of Musical Studies (AIMS), Graz, Austria.
~College Light Opera Company (CLOC), Falmouth, MA.

Voice Teacher
Blanche Thebom

Education
~ Oberlin College, 1989-93, B.A. Art History/Studio Art.
~ San Francisco Conservatory of Music, 1993-94.

Special Skills and Talents: Castanets, jaw harp, juggling, whistling, fencing, ballroom dance, tap dance, belly dance, stage-makeup, musical theater, painting, drawing, sculpting, accents, double-jointed in neck.

***

*** Charlotte O'Hara, Mezzo Soprano ***
(address, telephone etc..)

Erfahrung

Charlotte ~ Werther, San Francisco Lyric Opera, 1998.
Zerlina ~ Don Giovanni, Berkeley Opera, 1999.
Giulietta ~ King for a Day, (Verdi). Pocket Opera, San Francisco, 1999.
Secretary ~ The Consul, (Menotti), West Bay Opera, Palo Alto, 1999.
Nicklausse ~ Tales of Hoffmann, Pocket Opera, San Francisco, 1997-8.
Nancy ~ Martha, Pocket Opera, San Francisco, 1998.
Polinesso ~ Ariodante, (Konzert Fassung), Pocket Opera, San Francisco, 1997.
Judith ~ Wuornos, (neue Oper von Carla Lucero), Brava Künstlerinnen, San Francisco, 1998.
Mary Eastin ~ The Dreamers, (David Conte und Phillip Littel), Weltuhrauffführung Sonoma City Opera, 1996.
Second Lady ~ Die Zauberflöte, Berkely Opera, George Cleve, con., 1996.
Amoroso ~ The Bridge of Sighs, (Offenbach), Pocket Opera, San Francisco, 1995
Carmen ~ Carmen, San Francisco Opera Guild outreach program, 1996-97
Alice in Operaland, Festaufführung-Übertreffungsprogramm, Pocket Opera, 1996-8

Aufgeführte Solopartien in Folgenden Oratorien

~Midnight Mass, (Charpentier), Lakeside Presbyterian Church, San Francisco, 1998.
~Coronation Mass, (Mozart), Stanford Memorial Church, Palo Alto, 1998.
~The Messiah, (Händel) kurze Fassung, Concord, 1996.
~Missa Brevis in D Major, K. 194, (Mozart), Oberlin College Chor Tournée, 1992.
~Litanae Lauretanae, K. 195, (Mozart), Oberlin College Chor, 1991.

Liederkonzerte

~Glimmerglass Junge Künstler Solovortragserie, Cooperstown, NY, 1997.
~Noe Valley Konzertserie, Noe Valley Ministerium, San Francisco, 1996.

Preise und Auszeichnungen

~Teilnehmer-Ortsschlußrunde, Metropolitan Opera National Council Auditions, 1995.
~Erste Preis, Universität von Santa Clara Art Song Festival Competition, 1994.
~National Schlußrunde Preisträgerin, National Society of Arts and Letters, 1997.
~Preisträgerin, East Bay Opera League, Oakland, CA, 1999.

Musikprogramme
~Glimmerglass Opera Young American Artist Program, Cooperstown, NY.
~American Institute of Musical Studies (AIMS), Graz, Austria.
~College Light Opera Company (CLOC), Falmouth, MA.

Gesangslehrerin
Blanche Thebom

Ausbildung
~ Oberlin College, 1989-93, B.A. Kunstgeschichte/Atelierkunst.
~ San Francisco Conservatory of Music, 1993-94.

Besondere Kenntisse und Qualifizierungen: Kastanetten, Kieferharfe (jaw harp), Jonglieren, Pfeifen, Fechten, Tanzen, Stepptanzen, Bauchtanzen, Masken Bildnerin, Musical Theater, Malerei, Zeichnen, Bildhauerei, Fremdakzente, flexibel Hals.

***

Lebenslauf

Henry Stokes M.A. (Cantebury) L.R.A.M
geboren 1949 Wimbeldon, England
Staatsangehörigkeit: Britisch

Ausbildung

1960-68	Schüler des Gymnasiums Tiffin Boys School Kingston.
1968	Stipendiat an der Cambridge University, St. John's College.
1971-73	Weiterbildung in den Fächern Gesang, Querflöte und Dirigieren an der Royal Academy of Music, London.
1971	Diplom „Bachelor of Arts", Cambridge.
1973	Diplom „Licentiate of the Royal Academy of Music".
1975	Diplom „Master of Arts", Cambridge.

Lehrtätigkeiten und Auftritte

1976	Fachleiter für Musik am Thames Valley Sixth From College
1977	Lecturer of Music, Richmond Tertiary College
1974-80	Freischaffende Arbeit als Sänger und Dirigent. Mitglied der a capella-Gesangsgruppe "Counterpoint". Rege Konzerttätigkeit, u.a. auf den London Konzert-Bühnen Wigmore Hall, Purcell Room, und Queen Elisabeth Hall.
1996-97	Konzerte als Gastdirigent mit dem Philharmonischen Orchester Hagen und dem Lethmathe Oratorien Chor.
1980-99	Auftritte als Countertenor in den Bereichen „Oratorium und "Alte Musik" sowie Uraufführungen eigener Werke; daneben Bühnenauftritte.

***

Theaterlaufbahn

1980   Engagement als Korrepetitor mit Dirigierverpflichtung am Oldenburgischen Staatstheater.

1984   weiterverpflichtet in Oldenburg als Studienleiter und Kapellmeister.

1987   Engagement als Studienleiter und Kapellmeister an den Städtischen Bühnen, Freiburg.

1993   Engagement als Chordirektor und Kapellmeister am Stadttheater Hagen.

seit 1995   Engagement als Chordirektor und Kapellmeister am Theater Dortmund.

Dirigat:

*L'Incoronazione di Poppea, L'Ormiado, Così fan tutte, Showboat,
Hoffmanns Erzählungen, Wienerblut, Petruschka, Medea, Die
Verkaufte Braut, Feuervogel, Romeo und Julia* (Prokoviev),
*Manon, Der Schnee, Don Giovanni, Der Rosenkavalier, Tosca,
Werther, Liebestrank, Hänsel und Gretel, Il Trovatore,
Der Freischütz, Zar und Zimmermann, Die Lustigen Weiber von
Windsor, Cavalleria Rusticana, La Forza del Destino, Orpheus* (Gluck)

Einstudierung und Dirigate folgender Werke:

Prokoviev; *Peer Gynt* (Ballet)
Delibes; *Don Parasol* (Ballet)
Rameau; *Hippolyt et Aricie*
Halevy; *Der Blitz*
Schostakovich; *O Russland , du mein Volk* (Ballet)
Purcell; *König Artus*
Hindemith; *Cardillac*
Mozart; *Die Entführung aus dem Serail* (Wiederaufnahme)
Orff; *Carmina Burana*

***

LYRIK Künstleragentur
Inh. Irmgard Veress
Prof. Heiner Hopfner
Artilleriestr. 8 b
D-80636 München

Dortmund, den 4. März, 2000

Sehr geehrte Frau Veress und sehr geehrter Herr Professor Hopfner,

hiermit möchte ich mich vorstellen. Ich heiße Jane Doe und ich habe das Stimmfach Lyrischer Koloratur Sopran. Von 10. Oktober bis 15. Dezember werde ich mich in Deutschland aufhalten, und möchten Sie um einen Vorsingtermin bitten.

Ich lege meinen Lebenslauf bei, und stehe Ihnen gerne zur Verfügung.

Um eine positiv Antwort würde ich mich freuen und verbleibe mit freundlichen Grüßen,

xxxxxxxxxxxxxxxxxx

***

Translation:

Dear Ms Veress and Prof. Hopner,

I would like to introduce myself. My name is Jane Doe and I am a lyric coloratura soprano. I will be in Germany between October 10 and December 15, and would like to sing for you during this time.

Enclosed you will find a recent resumé, photo, and repertoire list.

I will look forward to hearing from you soon.

Sincerely,

XXXXXXXXXXXXXXXXXXXXX
(Keep it short!)

Chapter Three

Other Employment Opportunities in the German-Speaking Festsystem

When attempting to land a solo contract in a German-speaking theater, one should not rule out the possibility of a position in one of the nearly 100 opera and radio choruses throughout Germany, Austria, and Switzerland.

Don't believe the saying, "If anyone ever finds out you were in a chorus, they will never take you seriously as a soloist." First of all, "they" never have to know. Second, it simply isn't true. I (William) once read that Leo Nucci was in the La Scala opera chorus until he was nearly 35 years old. That blows that theory out of the water. Two of the soloists in my theater sang in opera choruses for nearly ten years before becoming soloists. It hasn't hurt their careers one bit.

There are great benefits that come with being in the chorus. First, believe it or not, in some of the larger houses, you will get paid *more* than you would as an *Anfänger* (beginner) *soloist*. Also, as a chorister, after two years, if you are "voted in," you are *unkündbar* (tenured). That's right, you have a job for life, if that is what you want.

Without a doubt, the most valuable part of starting out in the chorus is that *you learn German*. The Americans that we know and have observed over the years who presently sing or have sung in an opera chorus have an unusually good command of the German language.

Imagine the confidence they have when presenting themselves at an audition. This benefit cannot be overemphasized.

If you are not ruling out the possibility of singing in a chorus, make sure you let the agents know you would not object to auditioning for a chorus position. However, if what you really want is a solo contract, then wait until you have done a few house auditions. See whether or not they are successful, then decide where to go from there. Face it, some agents really have strange ears, and if you tell them at the beginning you would be willing to accept a chorus position, they may just assume you don't have what it takes to be a soloist. So, again, consider your options, think clearly, and then proceed.

Other jobs available in the German-speaking *Festsystem* are that of *Korrepetitor* (accompanist/coach), *Studienleiter* (basically, the head-*Korrepetitor* with administrative duties), *Korrepetitor mit Dirigierverpflichtung* (accompanist/coach with conducting duties), *Chorleiter* (Chorus Director), *Dirigent* (conductor) and *Souffleur* (prompter). It goes without saying that a prerequisite for these positions is an excellent command of the German language. If your language skills are not the best, and you still aspire to be an accompanist/coach, you might consider the position of *Ballet Korrepetitor*. That way you are at least in the system, thus in the country, and have an opportunity to learn the language and later "move up."

Just as a soloist and chorister, when pursuing these other musical opportunities as an instrumentalist, send your materials to the agents and request a *Vorspieltermin* (audition date).

***

A Word for Conductors:

An aspiring conductor should be realistic about his possibilities in the German-speaking theaters. The competition for you is even tougher than it is for singers. Therefore, most, if not all conductors begin as a *Korrepititor mit Dirigierverpflichtung* (accompanist/coach with conducting duties). This way, one learns the necessary repertoire through coaching and accompanying rehearsals, and also has the opportunity to conduct a few times a year. It is only then that the powers-that-be (almost always the orchestra), decide if you "have what it takes" to continue in this venue. It is usually easier to secure such a position in one of the many smaller to medium-size houses than in a larger "A" or "B" theater.

Once you have received a contract in a theater, you will have the opportunity to move up the ladder of the conducting hierarchy. The top-spot, of course, is that of the *GMD* or *Generalmusikdirektor.* (Now, do we really have to translate that one for you?) The second in command, so to speak, is the *1. Kapellmeister,* then the *2. Kapellmeister.* These positions vary in degrees of responsibility, depending upon the needs of each particular theater. You may take over the conducting responsibilities of an opera that is already running in the repertoire. In addition, as *1. Kapellmeister,* you are entitled to conduct one première per season. As *1.* or *2. Kapellmeister* you may also be put in the situation of conducting all of the musicals and/or ballets. If this is your specialty, then you are in luck. Even if it is not, it gives you a wonderful opportunity to be in front of the orchestra.

Chapter Four

The German Fachsystem

It is the opinion of many *fest* singers in Germany today that the German *Fachsystem* simply no longer exists. Some will say that this is a result of the extreme economic cutbacks in government funding of the theaters, thus forcing the engaged singers to sing several different *Fächer* (plural for *Fach*). Though economics has certainly played a major role in this change, another reason may be that many of those responsible for making casting decisions simply do not know the difference between a *Lyrischertenor* and a *Heldentenor*.

No one can deny that we presently live in a world of ever increasing visual orientation. It would be naive to assume that this influence has not flowed over into our own profession. Have you heard the expression, "They seem to be listening with their eyes, and not their ears"? This seems to occur quite frequently. So, if you think you look perfect for a certain role, play it up! Yes, at times, more often than not, singers seem to get hired based more on what they look like and NOT on how they sound.

This having been said, we have compiled a short list of repertoire requirements corresponding with each specific voice type, or *Fach*. For a more detailed list we recommend Rudolph Kloiber's *Handbuch der Oper*, which is a two-volume set, published by Bärenreiter. As you will notice, some *Fachs* cross lines, and some are quite clearcut. You will have to decide for yourself where you fit in, and how you want to present yourself, based on what suits your particular instrument.

The *Fächer* that you will have to contend with fall into two basic male and female categories. These categories are the "*Seriöse*" and "*Spiel*" or "*Charakter*" *Fächer*. Determining your *Fach* requires much consideration and advice from your coach and/or voice teacher. Keep in mind that your voice isn't the only consideration. Your language skills, physical appearance, and personality play a large role as well.

***

The German Fächer

Lyrischer Sopran : (c′ to c‴) a mellow, warm voice with beautiful "*Schmelz*" (a melting-point!) A lyrical, noble line.

Roles: *Michëla*, Carmen; *Gretel*, Hänsel und Gretel; *Susanna*, Figaro; *Zerlina*, Don Giovanni; *Pamina*, Die Zauberflöte; *Lauretta*, Gianni Schicchi.

Jugendlich-dramatischer Sopran: (c′ to c‴) a lyric-soprano voice, more voluminous and heavier. This voice-type is designed to sustain moments of high vocal drama.

Roles: Marie, *Wozzeck*; Magda Sorella, *The Consul*; Mimi, *La Bohème*; Butterfly, *Madame Butterfly*; Elisabeth, *Tannhäuser*; Eva, *Meistersinger*; Agathe, *Der Freischütz*.

Dramatischer Koloratursopran: (c′ to f‴) a flexible voice with a strong top, and dramatic sustaining power.

Roles: Norma, *Norma*; Donna Anna and Donna Elvira, *Don Giovanni*; Fiordiligi, *Così fan tutte*; Königin der Nacht, *Die Zauberflöte*; Leonora, *Il Trovatore*; Violetta, *La Traviata*.

Dramatischer Sopran: (g to c''') a voluminous, cutting, steely sound. Sustaining power.

Roles: Leonora, *Fidelio*; Tosca, *Tosca;* Turandot, *Turandot*; Salome, *Salome*; Ariadne, *Ariadne auf Naxos*; Lady Macbeth, *Macbeth*; Elisabeth, *Don Carlos*; Aida, *Aida;* Venus, *Tannhäuser;* Brünhilde, *Siegfried.*

Dramatischer Mezzosopran: (g to b'', also c''') a flexible, ringy "*Zwischen Fachstimme*" (between *Fachs*) voice, of a darker color, that with increasing maturity will one day develop into a "*Hochdramatisch*" *Fach.* Good top.

Roles: Secretary, *The Consul*; Herodias, *Salome*; Octavian, *Der Rosenkavalier*; Komponist, *Ariadne auf Naxos*; Preziosilla, *La Forza del Destino*; Eboli, *Don Carlos*; Kundry, *Parsifal*; Brangäne, *Tristan und Isolde.*

Dramatischer Alt: (g to b'') flexible, ringy-sounding voice, with well-developed top and chest; dramatic sustaining power.

Roles: Cornelia, *Julius Ceasar*; Lucia, *Cavalleria*; Mother, *The Consul*

Tiefer Alt (*Kontra Alt*): (f to a'') a full, luscious voice, with substantial chest (voice, that is).

Roles: (none listed)

Lyrischer Tenor: (c to d'') a lyrical, flexible voice with a long range and *schönem schmeltz* (a beautiful, velvety, ravishing quality).

Roles: Nadir, *The Pearl Fishers;* Albert, *Albert Herring*; Nemorino, *L'Elisir d'Amore*; Edgardo, *Lucia di Lammamoor*; Ernesto, *Don Pasquale*; Ottavio, *Don Giovanni*; Belmonte, *Die Entführung*; Tamino, *Die Zauberflöte*; Pinkerton, *Madame Butterfly*; Alfredo, *La Traviata;* Duke, *Rigoletto*; Casio, *Otello.*

Jugendlicher Heldentenor: (c to c″) a pingy instrument that can negotiate lyrical passages equally as well as dramatically challenging moments. Noble, tenoral color.

Roles: Don José, *Carmen*; Arturo, *Lucia di Lammamoor*; Chénier, *André Chénier*; Faust, *Faust*; Canio, *Pagliacci*; Idomeneo; *Idomeneo*; Cavaradossi, *Tosca*; Rodolfo, *La Bohème*; Macduff, *Macbeth*; Manrico, *Il Trovatore*; Don Carlos, *Don Carlos*; Don Alvaro, *La Forza del Destino*; Radamès, *Aida*; Parsifal, *Parsifal*; Lohengrin, *Lohengrin*.

Heldentenor: (c to c″) a heavy, voluminous voice with carrying power in the middle and bottom. This voice often has a baritone-ish quality to it.

Roles: Peter Grimes, *Peter Grimes*; Bacchus, *Ariadne auf Naxos*; Otello, *Otello*; Tannhäuser, *Tannhäuser*; Tristan, *Tristan und Isolde*; Siegfried, *Siegfried*.

Lyrischer Bariton: (B to a♭′) a smooth, lyric, flexible voice with beautiful line and a strong top.

Roles: Zurga, *The Pearl Fishers*; Belcore, *L'Elisir d'Amore*; Malatesta, *Don Pasquale*; Fluth, *Lustigen Weiber von Windsor*; Figaro, *Il Barbiere*; Dandini, *La Cenerentola*; Silvano, *Ballo in Maschera*.

Kavalierbariton: (A to g′) a ringy, biting voice, with legato sustaining power in both the top and bottom. Should possess a masculine, noble, baritonal quality.

Roles: Escamillo, *Carmen*; Enrico, *Lucia di Lammamoor*; Valentin, *Faust*; Il Conto, *Le Nozze di Figaro*; Giovanni, *Don Giovanni*; Marcello, *La Bohème*; Sharpless, *Madame Butterfly*; Renato, *Ballo in Maschera*; Posa, *Don Carlos*; Ford, *Falstaff*; Wolfram, *Tannhäuser*.

Heldenbariton: (occasionally called a High Bass) (G to f#′) a heavy, unusually huge instrument that not only has a stunningly ringing top, but also a great middle with carrying power and upper register to burn! Roles: Don Pizarro, *Fidelio*; Tonio, *Gli Pagliacci*; Jochanahan, *Salome*; Macbeth, *Macbeth*; Di Luna, *Il Trovatore*; Don Carlos, *La Forza del Destino*; Amonasro, *Aida*; Iago, *Otello*; Holländer, *Der Fliegender Holländer*; Kurvenal, *Tristan und Isolde*; Wotan, *Rheingold*; Amfortas/Klingsor, *Parsifal*.

Seriöser Baß (*Tiefer Baß*): (C to f′) a sonorous voice with a dark timbre, long range.

Roles: Rocco, *Fidelio*; Zuniga, *Carmen*; Raimondo, *Lucia di Lammamoor*; Bartolo, *Le Nozze di Figaro*; Commendatore, *Don Giovanni*; Colline, *La Bohème*; Sparafucile, *Rigoletto*; Ferrando, *Il Trovatore*; Pater, *La Forza del Destino*; King Phillip, *Don Carlos*; Landgraf, *Tannhäuser*; Marke, *Tristan und Isolde*; Gurnemanz, *Parsifal*; Sarastro, *Die Zauberflöte*.

***

Spiel- und Charakterfächer (Buffo and Character *Fach*s)

Lyrischer Koloratursopran: (c′ to f‴) a very flexible voice, long range, with supple and easy top.

Roles: Zerbinetta, *Ariadne auf Naxos*; Blondchen, *Die Entführung*; Norina, *Don Pasquale*; Marie, *The Daughter of the Regiment*; Lucia, *Lucia di Lammamoor*.

Spielsopran (*Soubrette*): (c′ to c‴) a delicate, malleable voice; petite appearance. It is essential that the singer have command of the German language for this *Fach*.

Roles: Gianetta, *L'Elisir d'Amore*; Adele, *Die Fledermaus*; Barbarina, *Le Nozze di Figaro*; Papagena, *Die Zauberflöte*; Marzellina, *Fidelio*; Ännchen, *Der Freischütz*; sometimes Musetta, *La Bohème*; Valencienne, *The Merry Widow*; Esmerelda, *The Bartered Bride*; sometimes Marie, *Zar und Zimmerman*.

Charaktersopran: (b to c''') a colorfully-timbred between-*Fach* voice that bridges the soprano and alto ranges. Excellent acting skills are necessary.
Roles: generally cast by directors' discretion.

Spielalt (Lyrischer Mezzosopran): (g to b♭') a supple, lithe sound, with a versatile vocal-acting capacity.
Roles: Florence Pike, *Albert Herring*; Nancy, *Martha*; Marcellina, *Le Nozze di Figaro*; Lola, *Cavalleria*; Meg Page, *Falstaff*.

Spieltenor (Tenorbuffo): (c to b') a slender, characterful voice.
Roles: Beppo, *Pagliacci*; Pedrillio, *Die Entführung*; Monostatos, *Die Zauberflöte*; Spoleta, *Tosca*; Goro, *Madame Butterfly*; Trabuco, *La Forza del Destino*; Bardolf, *Falstaff*.

Charaktertenor: (A to b') a between-*Fach* voice. Characterization capabilities.
Roles: Hauptmann, *Wozzeck*; Herodies, *Solome*; Guillot, *Manon*; Rudolf, *William Tell*; Mime, *Siegfried*; Loge/Mime, *Rheingold*; Dr. Caius, *Falstaff*.

Charakterbariton: (A to g') a strong, sturdy, moveable instrument. Refined characterization capabilites.
Roles: Wozzeck, *Wozzeck*; Peter, *Hänsel und Gretel*; Paolo, *Simone Boccanegra*; Beckmesser, *Meistersinger*; Rigoletto, *Rigoletto*; Shaunard, *La Bohème*; Scarpia, *Tosca*.

Spielbaß (Baßbuffo): (E to f′) a slender, flexible and characterful voice.

Roles: Leporello, *Don Giovanni*; Mesner, *Tosca*; Dulcamara, *L'Elisir d'Amore*; Pasquale, *Don Pasquale*; Don Alfonso, *Così fan Tutte*; Don Magnifico, *La Cenerentola*; Pistol, *Falstaff.*

Charakterbaß (Baßbariton): (E to f′) a big, full instrument. Refined acting skills a must.

Roles: Figaro, *Le Nozze di Figaro*; Masetto, *Don Giovanni*; Alidoro, *La Cenerentola*; Monterone, *Rigoletto*; Timur, *Turandot*; Bitterolf, *Tannhäuser*; Kothner, *Meistersinger.*

Schwerer Spielbaß (Schwerer Baßbuffo): (D to f′) a voluminous voice of great substance.

Roles: Mephistopheles, *Faust*; Osmin, *Die Entführung*; Falstaff, *Lustige Weiber*; Plumkett, *Martha*; Schicchi, *Gianni Schicchi*; Basilio, *Il Barbiere*; Ochs, *Der Rosenkavalier*; Daland, *Der Fliegender Holländer.*

"One of the most important things a singer can do is to contact every agent, and try to sing for as many of them as possible."

Kammersänger Andreas Becker, Bass Baritone
Stadttheater Dortmund

Chapter Five

Agents

The following list of agents is perhaps the most important information you can have. We have tried to be as accurate as possible and apologize in advance for any changes in telephone or fax numbers. It is our strong opinion that you should contact *every* agent initially *by mail only*. Of course send them a recent photo, preferably postcard-size: 4 x 6 (this can be done quickly and efficiently at any of the photo labs in your own home town or your neighborhood Kinko's), resumé, biography, repertoire list, and reviews.

Some of your teachers and coaches may disagree with this, but unless your German letters are written perfectly, please send a three-sentence letter in English requesting a *Vorsingtermin* (audition time). We believe you should write the agents no later than the month of June, asking for an audition in September or October. Normally, the theaters' seasons end in June or July (depending on the *Bundesland* [state]). August is traditionally a "closed shop" (vacation) month. Please remember, by October, most theaters know which artists they will be keeping and those they will be letting go for the following season.

Note: Feel free to contact the agents at any time of the year. Your materials may actually get more attention when the agents are not so swamped with others' resumés. Likewise, don't assume that you will get lots of auditions just because you are here during the fall months. Case in point: A tenor friend of ours came over in 1998 for a three-week audition tour. He stayed during the traditionally peak time for auditioning, November. He garnered *only one house audition* during his stay. Of course, when he returned to the States, he was called back here to do three more house auditions. Lesson learned: Plan no less than six to ten weeks for your audition tour. You can *always* fly home early, should you land a position or tire of the rain.

Something to consider:

Just as the German Telekom phone system was deregulated in 1998, one could say that the opera-agency industry has been deregulated recently as well. It is very inexpensive to "set up shop." *As a result, there are now nearly 50 agents in the German-speaking countries for whom one could feasibly.* In comparison, ten years ago one would sing for only eight to ten. There are two ways to view this: Either there are a lot more opportunities, or a lot more people in the business who know little about singing. We will let you decide for yourself.

A word about the ZBF:

The *Zentrale Bühnen, Fernseh-und Filmvermittlung* or *ZBF* is a division of Germany's *Arbeitsamt* (Department of Labor). If you have the time, it wouldn't hurt to sing for them at each of their locations. Remember, one agent may love you one day, and another not care for you the next. Write directly to *ZBF* as you would any of the private agencies. The following is an up-to-date list of agents in the German-speaking countries.

***

Agents in the German-speaking Countries
Zentrale Bühnen-, Fernseh-und Filmvermittlung

ZBF
Generalagentur Bonn
Villemombler Straße 76
D-53123 Bonn
Tel. 0228/713-0, Fax 0228/713-1349
E-mail: *zbf.bonn.the@t-online.de*

ZBF
Agentur Berlin
Ordenmeisterstraße 15
D-12099 Berlin
Tel. 030/75760-0, Fax 030/75760-249
E-Mail: *zbf.berlin@t-online.de*

ZBF
Agentur Hamburg
Kreuzweg 7
D-20099 Hamburg
Tel. 040/284015-0, Fax 040/284015-99
E-Mail: *zbf.hamburg.the@t-online.de*

ZBF
Agentur München
Leopoldstraße 19
D-80802 München
Tel. 089/381707-0, Fax 089/381707-38
E-Mail: *zbf.muenchen@t-online.de*

ZBF
Agentur Leipzig
Georg-Schumann-Straße 173
D-04159 Leipzig
Tel. 0341/58088-0, Fax 0341/58088-50
E-Mail: *zbf.leipzig@t-online.de*

***

Other German-Licensed Agencies

Agentur für Musiktheater und Konzert
Hannagret Bueker
Fuhsestraße 2
D-30419 Hannover
Tel. 0511/271 69 10
Fax 0511/271 78 73

Opern- und Konzertagentur
Lore Blümel
Postanschrift: Postfach 17 25
D-82159 Gräfelfing
Büro: Pasinger Straße 28
D-82152 Planegg
Tel. 089/8 59 38 64
Fax 089/8 59 37 59
E-Mail: *opkoag-bluemel@t-online.de*

Musikthater und Konzert In- und Ausland
Marianne Böttger
Dahlmannstraße 9
D-10629 Berlin
Tel. 030/ 3 24 85 27

Fax 030/ 3 23 11 93
E-Mail: *agency@boettger-berlin.de*
Homepage: *http://www.boettger-berlin.de*

Musiktheater und Konzert In- und Ausland
Reinald Heissler-Remy
Mitarbeiter: Neill Thornborrow
Postfach 11 09 31
D-40509 Düsseldorf
Street address:
Drakestraße 2
D-40545 Düsseldorf
Tel. 0211/57 80 51
Fax 0211 55 34 98
E-Mail: *remy.agent@t-online.de*

Vermittlung für Musiktheater und Konzert
Dr. Germinal Hilbert
Mitarbeiter: Rudolf Meindl
Maximilianstraße 22
D-80539 München
Tel. 089/ 29 07 47-0
Fax 089/ 29 07 47- 90
E-Mail: *agentur@hilbert.de*

Marguerite Kollo
Rüsternallee 19
D-14050 Berlin
Tel. 030/30 10 00 14
Fax 030/30 10 00 15

Werner Kühnly
Mitarbeiterin: Herta Kühnly
Wörthstraße 31
D-70563 Stuttgart
Tel. 0711/ 7 80 27 64
Fax 0711/ 7 80 44 03
E-Mail: *Kuenhly@aol.com*

Theateragentur Glado von May
Mitarbeiterin: Heidi Schäfer
Hermannstraße 32
D-60318 Frankfurt a.M.
Tel. 069/ 28 33 47
Fax 069/ 29 55 13

Günther Ocklenburg
Mitarbeiter: Wolfgang Schmitt
Hartungstraße 15
D-20146 Hamburg
Tel. 040/ 41 86 56 and 41 01 494
Fax 040/ 4 10 46 68

Sigrid Rostock
Eugen-Schönhaar-Straße 1
D-10407 Berlin
Tel. 030/ 4 25 75 14
Fax 030/ 4 23 91 36

Opernagenturin Inge Tennigkeit
Kempner Str. 4
D-40474 Düsseldorf

Tel. 0211/ 516 00 60
Fax 0211/ 51 60 06 16

Konzert-Direktion Hans Adler
Inh.: Witiko Adler
Auguste-Viktoria-Straße 64
D-14199 Berlin
Tel. 030/ 8 25 63 33
Fax 030/8 26 35 20
E-Mail: *info@musikadler.de*
Homepage: *www.musikadler.de*

ALLEGRO Artist Management
Direktor: Pekka K. Pohjola
Mitarbeiterin: Anne-Kathrin Seibel and Vilja Valkeinen
Alexander Plaza Berlin WWBC
Rosenstrasse 2
D-10178 Berlin
Tel. 030/24 31 02 166
Fax 030/24 31 02 594
E-Mail: *allegroberlin@sireconnect.de*

Bellegato Künstlermanagement
Sofia Simmons (vorm. Franz Hajtas)
Freiburger Str. 1/2
D-69126 Heidelberg
Tel. 06221/ 37 43 02
Fax 06221/ 37 26 90
E-mail: *Bellegato@hotmail.com*

Künstleragentur Petra Breidenbach
Schleifweg 11

D-90409 Nürnberg
Tel. 0911/ 3 50 93 10
Fax 0911/ 3 50 93 11

Künstleragentur Helge Rudolf Augustein
Sebastiansplatz 3
D-80331 München
Tel. 089/ 26 02 43 33
Fax 089/ 26 02 43 44
E-Mail: Agentur *HRA@aol.com*

Theateragentur Leipzig
Inh. MD Wolfgang Hoyer
Brandvorwerkstr. 78
D-04275 Leipzig
Tel. 0341/301 83 18
Fax 0341/391 86 11

"Culture-Consulting"
Michael Fuger, Karin Fuger
Soonblick 8
D-55543 Bad Kreuznach
Tel. 0671/ 8 96 42 70
Fax 0671/ 8 96 42 40

Cecilia Musik Concept GmbH
Franz-Georg Stähling (Geschf.)
Am Eichenwäldchen 23
D-50996 Köln
Tel. 02236/ 6 23 29
Fax 02236/ 6 23 91

Konzert Direktion Fritz Dietrich
Eckenheimer Landstraße 483
D-60435 Frankfurt a. Main
Tel. 069/ 54 45 04 and 54 56 68
Fax 069/ 5 48 41 07

Opern- und Konzertagentur
Monika Bundschu
Tal 15
D-80331 München
Tel. 089/ 29 16 16 63
Fax 089/ 29 16 16 67

Dietrich Eberhard Gross, Künstleragentur
Eschenweg 19
D-61440 Oberusel
Tel. 06172/ 93 41 44
Fax 06172/ 93 41 45
E-Mail: *D.E.Gross@t-online.de*
Homepage: *home.t-online.de/home/d.e.gross*

Artists Management Hartmut Haase
Aalgrund 8
D-31275 Lehrte
Tel. 05175/ 95 32 32
Fax 05175/ 95 32 33
E-Mail: *artists@t-online.de*

International Künstleragentur EYHXON
Athanasios Oikonomou
Menzingerstr. 21
D-80638 München

Tel. 089/ 17 09 40 79
Fax 089/ 17 09 40 81

Barbara Güzlow
Lucia-Popp-Bogen 17
D-81245 München
Tel. 089/ 86 30 86 37
Fax 089/ 86 30 86 38

Herwald Artists
Thomas Herwald, Inhaber
Strasse des Roten Kreuzes 64
D-76228 Karlsruhe
Tel. 0721/ 947 39 39
Fax 0721/ 947 39 37
E-Mail: *Herwald-artists@t-online.de*

Norddeutsche Konzertdirektion Melsine Grevesmühl
Postfach 31 02 65
D-27538 Bremerhaven
Tel. 0471/ 8 80 68
Fax 0471/ 8 80 60
E-Mail: *grevesmuehlballet@t-online.de*

Brigitte Jagusch
Kurfürstendamm 142
D-10709 Berlin
Tel. 030/ 312 70 78
Fax 030/ 313 42 24

Lyrik Künstleragentur e.K.
Inh. Irmgard Veress

Mitarbeiter: Prof. Heiner Hopfer
Artilleriestr. 8 b
D-80636 München
Tel. 089/ 1 23 88 50
Fax 089/ 12 74 95 75
E-Mail: *IrmgardV@t-online.de*

Dr. Carl F. Jickeli
Nymphenburger Str. 62
D-80335 München
Tel. 089/ 12 39 26 26
Fax 089/ 12 39 26 27

Manuela Kursdem &Elene Tschaisde
Opern & Konzertagentur
Michael Lewin, Künstlermanagement
Tal 15
D-80331 München
Tel. 089/ 29 16 16 61 and 29 16 16 62
Fax 089/ 29 1616 67

in Berlin:
Mitabeiterin: J. Bredtmeyer
Maassenstr. 14 D-10777 Berlin
Tel. 030/ 2 16 82 14
Fax 030/ 2 15 97 76
Austrian address:
Wasagasse 12/1/A-1090 Wien

Konzertdirektion Hans Ulrich Schmid
Schmiedestraße 8
D-30159 Hannover

Tel. 0511/ 3 66 07 77 and 3 66 07 33
Fax 0511/ 3 66 07 34
E-Mail: *Mail@KDSchmid.de*

Konzertdirektion Erich Schmidtke
Inh. Evelyne Schmidtke-Lennert
eigene Operettenproduction Johann-Strauß-Operetta Wien
Vogelsbergstr. 11
D-34131 Kassel
Tel + Fax 0561/ 31 57 32
Austrian address:
Pfauengasse 8/24
A-1060 Wien
Tel. + Fax 43 (0)1 5 86 55 07

Heidi Steinhaus
Tel. 089/ 93 93 01 10
Fax 089/ 93 93 01 11
E-Mail: *HeidiSteinhaus@aol.com*

Künstler Agentur Langosch
Bautzner Straße 18
D-10199 Dresden
Tel. 0351/ 8 02 23 00
Fax 0351/ 8 02 23 01
E-Mail: *AgenturLangosch@s-direktnet.de*

Boris Orlob
Jägerstraße 70
D-10177 Berlin
Tel. 030/ 204 508 39

Fax 030/ 204 508 49
E-Mail: *Boris_Orlob@compuserve.com*

Lore-M. Schulz
Zittlerstr. 8
D-80796 München
Tel. 089/ 308 70 92
Fax 089/ 308 70 93
E-Mail: *loreschulz.artists@t-online.de*

Elizabeth Seifert
Waltharistraße 32 B
D-14109 Berlin
Tel. 030/ 804 021 07
Fax 030/ 804 021 08

Wolfgang Stoll
Mitarbeiter: Karl-Erich Haase
Martiusstraße 4
D-80802 München
Tel. 089/ 33 31 62 and 39 41 90
Fax 089/ 34 26 74

Peter Seyfferth Artist Management
Walsroder Straße 148
D-30853 Langenhager/Hannover
Tel. 0511/ 73 93 30
Fax 0511/ 73 93 32
E-Mail: *PSeyfferth@gmx.net*
Hompage: *www.seyfferth.de*

Viartis Artist Management
Blumenplatz 3
D-79400 Kandern
Tel/Fax 07626 1351

Elke Wiemer
Badstraße 20, linker Seitenflügel
D-13357 Berlin
Tel. 030/ 494 65 08
Fax 030/ 493 53 33

Astrid K. Winkler
Ks. Hermann Winkler
Grillparzerstraße 46
D-81675 München
Tel. 089/ 4 70 58 57
Fax 089/ 4 70 71 23

Ilse Zellermayer
Schlüterstraße 54
D-10629 Berlin
Tel. 030/ 8 85 44 11
Fax 030/ 8 85 44 22

***

Austrian (country code: 43) and Swiss Agencies (country code: 41)

Remember: When dialing within the country, use the "0" but do not use the country code. When dialing from one country to another, dial "00" before the country code and drop the "0" after the country code. If you are still not clear about dialing to these countries, refer to chapter eight.

Italartist Austroconcert
Gluckgasse 1
A-1010 Wien
Tel. 43(0) 1-513-26 57
Fax 43(0) 1-512-61 54
E-Mail: *aconcert@magnet.at*

Künstleragentur Dr. Raab & Dr. Böhm
Plankengasse 7
A-1010 Wien
Tel. 43(0) 1 5 12 05 01
Fax 43(0) 1 5 12 77 43
E-Mail: *raab.boehm@magnet.at*

John Goodman
Dopschstraße 20/3
A- 1210 Wien
Tel. 43(0) 1 259-20-27
Fax 43(0) 1 259 61 24
E-Mail: *johngoodman@goodman.at*
Hompage: *www.goodman.at*

Künstleragentur
Hollaender-Calix
Grinzinger Allee 46
A-1190 Wien
Tel. 43 (0) 1 328 47 33
Fax 43 (0) 1 320 53 17
Fax 43 (0) 1 328 90 70

Kancz, Kathry, Kulturmanagement
Josephsteig 20
A-3400 Klosterneuburg
Tel. 43 (0) 1 315 53 04
Fax 43 (0) 1 319 09 18
E-Mail: *kulturmanagement@netway.at*

Promusica
Alexander Jankow
Postfach 38
A-1043 Wien
Tel. 43 (0) 1 503 65 75
Fax 43 (0) 1 505 30 80

Erich Seitter
Mitarbeiter: Mag. Kurt W. Schober
Opernring 8
A-1010 Wien
Tel. 43 (0) 1 5 13 75 92 and 5 13 75 93
Fax 43 (0) 1 5 12 93 51
E-Mail: *agentur.seitter@aon.at*

Lotte Vladarski
Mitarbeiter: Walter Vladarski
Reithleg. 12
A-1190 Wien
Tel. 43 (0) 1 3 68 69 60 and 3 68 69 61
Fax. 43 (0) 1 3 68 69 62
E-Mail: *opera.vladarski@netway.at*

Caecilia
Marino Horak
Stephanie Ammann
Rennweg 15
CH-800 Zürich
Tel. 41 (0) 1 2 21 33 88
Fax 41 (0)1 2 11 71 82
E-Mail: *caecilia@caecilia-lyric.ch*

Verena Keller, Artists Management
Lohwisstrasse 52
CH-8123 Ebmatingen (Zürich)
Tel. 41 (0) 1 980 15 13
Fax 41 (0) 1 980 36 86
E-Mail: *verena.keller@wdtnet.ch*

Concord Opera Management AG
Elisabeth Promonti
Micahel Suaser
Schaffhauserstr. 43
CH-8006 Zürich
Tel. 41 (0) 1 350 49 81
Fax 41 (0) 1 350 44 32

Pro Musica Classic GmbH
Konzert und Gastspielorganization
Postfach 27
CH-3000 Bern 15
Tel. 41 (0) 31 944 10 11
Fax 41 (0) 31 944 10 12

"*To the young American singer, I can only say they should judge and trust their gifts without paying too much attention to the remarks and observations of others. The importance of going one's own way and being true to one's self cannot be over emphasized.*"

Kammersänger Dietrich Fischer-Diskau, Baritone

Chapter Six

German-Speaking Theaters

This is an exhaustive list of German-speaking opera houses that have *"fest"* ensembles. (Remember, *"fest"* means salaried or full-time.) This information can also be found in the 2000 edition of the *Deutsches Bühnen-Jahrbuch*, published by the *Genossenschaft Deutscher Bühnen Angehöriger*. Their address is:

Genossenschaft Deutscher Bühnen-Angehöriger
Postfach 13 02 70
D-20102 Hamburg
Telephone: (040) 44 51 85
Fax: (040) 45 60 62

In reference to the "class" rating:

Do not be fooled by the class rating. It does not reflect the caliber of singers in any given opera house. It is simply a rating given to each house orchestra based on pay scale and the number of musicians in the orchestra. Ask anyone who has sung in Germany, and they will tell you that they have sung with singers in "A" houses who sing at the level of mediocre freshmen entering college. Likewise, we have performed in "C" houses with recording artist calibre singers who should or could be singing at the Met.

Included are also the theater's telephone and fax numbers. Some of these phone numbers are directly connected to the *Künstlerisches Betriebsbüro* or *KBB* (artistic administrator's office), and some are not.

We *do not* recommend calling the *KBB* directly unless you have been asked to do so, or if you have an audition scheduled and want to confirm the date and time. Assume that each theater thinks of itself as a little "Met." Then, just imagine calling directly to James Levine's office and asking for an audition.

Also, don't believe anyone who tells you not to bother sending your materials directly to a theater. There are countless numbers of singers who received their first *Festvertrag* (annual contract) by writing or faxing the theater(s) directly.

Names of hotels recommended by each theater, as well as their numbers have been included. As of this writing we have confirmed each telephone number. When auditioning, always tell the hotel that you are a guest of that town's particular theater, and they will often give you a discounted rate.

***

Theater Aachen
Hubertstraße 2-8
D-52064 Aachen
Tel: (0241) 4784-1
Fax: (0241) 4784-200
Seats: 871
Class: B
Hotel: Aquis Grana (0231) 44 30

Landestheater Altenburg
Theaterplatz 19
D-04600 Altenburg
Tel: (0365) 82 79 -0

Fax:
Seats: 555
Class: B
Hotel: Park Hotel (0365) 58 30

Theater Annaberg
Buchlotzerstraße 67
D-09456 Annaberg
Tel: (03733) 1407-0
Fax: (03733) 1407-8
Seats: 300
Class: D
Hotel: Wildemann (03733) 14 40

Theater Augsburg
Kasernstraße 4-6
D-86152 Augsburg
Tel: (0821) 324 4907
Fax: (0821) 324 4521
Seats: 975
Class: B
Hotel: Dom Hotel (0821) 153 031

Deutsche Staatsoper Berlin
Unter der Linden
D-10117 Berlin
Tel: (030) 203 54-210
Fax: (030) 203 540206
Seats: 1396
Class: A
Hotel: Hotel Am Gendarmen Markt (030) 203 750

Deutsche Oper Berlin
Bismarkstraße 35
D-10627 Berlin
Tel: (030) 343 8401
Fax: (030) 343 84 232
Seats: 1865
Class: A
Hotel: Frühling am Zoo (030) 881 8083
    Crystal Hotel (030) 31 290 47

Komische Oper Berlin
Behrenstraße 55-57
D-10117 Berlin
Tel: (030) 202 600
Fax: (030) 202 60 405
Seats: 1270
Class: A
Hotel: Kubrat Hotel (030) 201 2055

Theater Bielefeld
Brunnenstraße 3-9
D-33602 Bielefeld
Tel: (0521) 51 25 01
Fax: (0521) 51 64 54
Seats: 775
Class: B
Hotel: Merkur am Niederwall (0521) 52 53 0

Theater Bonn
Am Boeselagerhof 1
D-5311 Bonn
Tel: (0228) 77 8204

Fax: (0228) 77 8244
Seats: 1038
Class: A
Hotel: Hotel Savoy (0228) 72 59 70

Brandenburg Theater, GmbH
Grabenstraße 14
D-14776 Brandenburg
Tel: (03381) 511 0
Fax: (03381) 511 160
Seats: 300
Class: C
Hotel: City Hotel (03381) 52 26 92

Braunschweig Staatstheater
Am Theater
D-38100 Braunschweig
Tel: (0531) 12 34 -112
Fax: (0521) 12 34 -114
Seats: 903
Class: A
Hotel: Courtyard bei Mariott (0531) 48 14 0

Bremer Theater
Am Goetheplatz 1-3
D-28203 Bremen
Tel: (0421) 3653 212
Fax: (0421) 3653 601
Seats: 916
Class: A
Hotel: Hotel Weltervreden (0421) 78 015

Bremerhaven Stadttheater
Theodor-Heuss-Platz
D-27519 Bremerhaven
Tel: (0471) 48 21 62 88
Fax: (0471) 48 20 64 82
Seats: 722
Class: C
Hotel: An der Karlstadt (0471) 42 021

Städtische Theater Chemnitz
Käthe-Kollwitz-Straße 7
D-09111 Chemnitz
Tel: (0371) 69 69 810
Fax: (0371) 69 69 699
Seats: 714
Class: A
Hotel: Merkur Hotel (0371) 68 30

Landestheater Coburg
D-96450 Coburg
Tel: (09561) 88 522
Fax:
Seats: 557
Class: C
Hotel: Goldener Anker (09561) 55 7 00

Staatstheater Cottbus
Karl-Liebknecht-Straße
D-03046 Cottbus
Tel: (0355) 78 24 144
Fax: (0355) 79 13 33
Seats: 640

Class: B
Hotel: Sorat Hotel (0355) 78 440

Darmstadt Staatstheater
Marienplatz 2
D-64283 Darmstadt
Tel: (06151) 2811 316
Fax: (06151) 2811 226
Seats: 956
Class: A
Hotel: Hotel am Theater (06151) 29 69 05

Anhaltisches Theater Dessau
Friedenplatz 1a
D-06844 Dessau
Tel: (0340) 251 10
Fax: (0340) 251 12 13
Seats: 1096
Class: B
Hotel: Steigenberger (0340) 25 15 0

Detmold Landestheater
Theaterplatz 1
D-32756 Detmold
Tel: (05231) 974 60
Fax: (05231) 974 701
Seats: 676
Class: B
Hotel: Detmolder Hof (05231) 991 20

Theater Dortmund
Kuhstraße 12

D-44137 Dortmund
Tel: (0231) 50 224 56
Fax: (0231) 50 224 79
Seats: 1170
Class: A
Hotel: Hotel Astron (0231) 90 55 0

Dresden Semperoper
Theaterplatz 2
D-01067 Dresden
Tel: (0351) 49 11 0
Fax: (0351) 49 11 401
Seats: 1309
Class: A+
Hotel: Ibis Hotel Bastei (0351) 485 63 88

Deutsche Oper am Rhein
(Düsseldorf-Duisberg)
Heinrich Heine Allee 16a
D-40213 Düsseldorf
Tel: (0211) 89 08 0
Fax: (0211) 32 90 51
Seats: Opernhaus Düsseldorf-1342
 Duisberg Theater-1118
Class: A
Hotel: Hotel an der Oper (0211) 323 06 21

Thüringer Landestheater GmbH
Theaterplatz 4-7
D-99817 Eisenach
Tel: (03691) 256 0
Fax: (03691) 256 1 59

Seats: 635
Class: C
Hotel: Galleria Hotel (03691) 29570

Theater Erfurt
Walkmühstraße 13
D-99084 Erfurt
Tel: (0361) 22 33 0
Fax: (0361) 22 33 120
Seats: 700
Class: B
Hotel: Radison Hotel (0361) 55 10 294

Essen Theater
Opernplatz 10
D-45128 Essen
Tel: (0201) 81 22 220
Fax: (0201) 81 22 280
Seats: 1125
Class: A
Hotel: Sheraton (0201) 10070

Schleswig-Holsteinisches Landestheater
Rathausstraße 22
D-24937 Flensburg
Tel: (0461) 141 00 0
Fax: (0461) 141 00 83
Sears: 507
Class: B
Hotel: Hotel Central (0461) 86 00 0

Frankfurt Oper
Untermainanlage 11
D-60311 Frankfurt am Main
Tel: (069) 212 37 312
Fax: (069) 212 37 518
Seats: 1387
Class: A+
Hotel: Hotel am Dom (069) 28 21 41

Theater Freiberg
Borngasse 1
D-09599 Freiberg
Tel: (03731) 35 82 0
Fax: (03731) 23 4 06
Seats: 315
Class: C
Hotel: Pension am Dom (03721) 21111
        Hotel am Obermarkt (03721) 34361

Theater Freiburg
Bertoldstraße 46
D-79098 Freiburg
Tel: (0761) 201 2921
Fax: (0761) 201 2903
Seats: 906
Class: B
Hotel: Minerva Hotel (0761) 20 20 616

Theater Gelsenkirchen
(see Wuppertal)

Gera Theater
(see Altenburg)

Stadttheater Gießen
Berlinerplatz
D-35390 Gießen
Tel: (0641) 79 57 13
Fax: (0641) 79 57 80
Seats: 651
Class: D
Hotel: Am Ludwigplatz (0641) 93 11 30

Theater Görlitz
Demianplatz 2
D-02826 Görlitz
Tel: (03581) 47 47 33
Fax: (03581) 47 47 36
Seats: 640
Class: B
Hotel: Sorat Hotel (03581) 40 65 77

Vorpommersche Theater
(Greifswald/Stralsund)
Anklamerstraße 106
D-17489 Greifswald
Tel: (03834) 57 22 200
Fax: (03834) 57 22 242
Seats: 470
Class: B
Hotel: Europa Hotel (03834) 80 10

Theater Hagen
Elberstraße 65
D-58095 Hagen
Tel: (02331) 207 32 36
Fax: (02331) 207 24 46
Seats: 801
Class: B
Hotel: Hotel Lex (02331) 28 7 51

Nordharzer Stätdtbundtheater
(Halberstadt/Quedlinburg)
Spiegelstraße 20a
D-38820 Halberstadt
Tel: (03941) 69 65 0
Fax: (03941) 44 26 52
Seats: 501
Class: D
Hotel: Park Hotel (03941) 6000 77

Halle Opernhaus
Universitätsring 24
D-06108 Halle (Saale)
Tel: (0345) 51 10 104
Fax: (0345) 51 10 106
Seats: 672
Class: A
Hotel: Martha Haus (0345) 510 80

Hamburgische Staatsoper
Große Theaterstraße 34
D-20354 Hamburg
Tel: (040) 35 68 390

Fax: (040) 35 68 456
Seats: 1675
Class: A
Hotel: Marriot (040) 35 05 0
     Baseler Hof (040) 35 90 60
     Ramada (040) 34 9 180

Hannover Staatsoper
Opernplatz 1
D-30159 Hannover
Tel: (0511) 99 99 1020
Fax: (0511) 99 99 1920
Seats: 1207
Class: A
Hotel: Kastens Luisenhof (0511) 30 440

Heidelberg Stadttheater
Friedrichstraße 5
D-69117 Heidelberg
Tel: (0621) 58 3506
Fax: (0621) 58 3599
Seats: 619
Class: B
Hotel: City Hotel (0621) 291 18

Hildesheim Stadttheater
Theaterstraße 6
D-31141 Hildesheim
Tel: (05121) 16 93 0
Fax: (05121) 16 93 92
Seats: 597

Class: D
Hotel: Bürgermeister Kapelle (05121) 14 0 21

Hof (Saale) Städtebundtheater
Kulmbacherstraße 5
D-95030 Hof (Saale)
Tel: (09281) 70 70 0
Fax: (09281) 70 70 299
Seats: 567
Class: B
Hotel: Hotel Central (09182) 6050
Quality Inn (09281) 7030

Kaiserslautern Pfalztheater
Willy-Brandt-Platz 4-5
D-67655 Kaiserslautern
Tel: (0631) 36 75 0
Fax: (0631)
Seats: 730
Class: B
Hotel: Felsenhof (0631) 36 2 400

Karslruhe Badisches Theater
Baumeisterstraße 11
D-76137 Karlsruhe
Tel: (0721) 35 57 216
Fax: (0721) 35 32 23
Seats: 1002
Class: A
Hotel: Blankenburg Hotel (0721) 93 26 90

Kassel Staatstheater
Friedrichplatz 15
D-34117 Kassel
Tel: (0561) 10 94 122
Fax: (0561) 10 94 204
Seats: 953
Class: A
Hotel: Hotel am Rathaus (0561) 137 68

Kiel Bühnen der Landeshauptstadt
D-24015 Kiel
Tel: (0431) 901 2890
Fax: (0431) 901 628 89
Seats: 866
Class: B
Hotel: Name? 986 800

Koblenz Stadttheater
Clemenstraße 5
D-56068
Tel: (0261) 129 2805
Fax: (0261) 129 2800
Seats: 464
Class: B
Hotel: Trierer Hof (0261) 100 60

Köln Stadttheater
Offenbachplatz
D-50667 Köln
Tel: (0221) 221 0
Fax: (0221) 221 284 87
Seats: 1346

Class: A
Hotel: Ariane Hotel (0221) 23 60 33

Krefeld Stadttheater
Theaterplatz 3
D-47798 Krefeld
Tel: (02151) 805 114
Fax: (02151) 805 137
Seats: 830
Class: B
Hotel: Post Stuben (02151) 85 870
      Wilma Hotel (02151) 25 23 2

Oper Leipzig
August 12
D-04109 Leipzig
Tel: (0341) 1261 0
Fax: (0341) 960 58 51
Seats: 1422
Class: A
Hotel: Hotel Mercure (0341) 21 46 0

Lübecker Theater GmbH
Beckergrube 16
D-23552 Lübeck
Tel: (0451) 7088 118
Fax: (0451) 7088 119
Seats: 792
Class: B
Hotel: Radison (0451) 14 20

Theater Lüneburg
An der Reeperbahn 3
D-21335 Lüneburg
Tel: (04131) 752 215
Fax: (04131) 40 42 10
Seats: 542
Class: D
Hotel: Roten Tor (04131) 43 0 41

Theater der Hauptstadt Magdeburg
Universitätsplatz 9
D-39104 Magdeburg
Tel: (0391) 540 65 00
Fax: (0391) 540 65 99
Seats: 688
Class: B
Hotel: Ratsvaage (0391) 59 26 193

Staatstheater Mainz GmbH
Gutenbergplatz 7
D-55116 Mainz
Tel: (06131) 28 51 102
Fax: (06131) 28 51 109
Seats: 776
Class: B
Hotel: City Hotel (06131) 23 22 37
        Hof Ehrenfels (06131) 22 43 34

Mannheim Nationaltheater
Am Goetheplatz
D-68161 Mannheim
Tel: (0621) 16 80 0

Fax: (0621) 16 80 388
Seats: 1154
Class: A
Hotel: Mack Hotel (0621) 124 20

Mönchengladbach Stadttheater
Odenkirchenerstraße 78
D-41236 Mönchengladbach
Tel: (02166) 61 51 0
Fax: (02166) 42 01 10
Seats: 811
Class: B
Hotel: Hotel zur Post (02166) 47 023

Bayrische Staatsoper
Nationaltheater Briefach
D-80075 München
Tel: (089) 21 85 01
Fax: (089) 21 85 11 33
Seats: 2100
Class: A
Hotel: Hotel an der Oper (089) 29 00 270
        Hotel am Markt (089) 22 50 14

Staatstheater am Gärtnerplatz
Gärtnerplatz 3
D-80469 München
Tel: (089) 202 41 1
Fax: (089) 202 41 237
Seats: 893
Class: B
Hotel: Hotel Appart (089) 620 390

Stadttheater Münster
Neubrückenstraße 63
D-48143 Münster
Tel: (0251) 59 09 118
Fax: (0251) 59 09 105
Seats: 955
Class: B
Hotel: Coerde Hof (0251) 92 20 20

Landestheater Mecklenburg, Neustrelitz
D-17235 Neustrlelitz
Tel: (03981) 277 0
Fax: (03981) 20 54 35
Seats: 397
Class: B(Neubrandenburg Philharmonic)
Hotel: Park Hotel (03981) 48 900

Nordhausen Theater
Käthe Kollwitz Straße 15
D-99734
Tel: (03631) 6 26 00
Fax: (03631) 626 0147
Seats: 488
Class: B
Hotel: Avena (03631) 60 20 60

Theater Nürnberg
William Wagner Platz 2-10
D-90443 Nürnberg
Tel: (0911) 231 35 75
Fax: (0911) 231 35 22
Seats: 1074

Class: A
Hotel: Deutsche Hof (0911) 249 40

Oldenburg Staatstheater
Theaterwall 28
D-26122 Oldenburg
Tel: (0441) 22 25 0-
Fax: (0441)
Seats: 827
Class: B
Hotel: Hotel Wieting (0441) 924 005

Osnabrück Stadttheater
Domhof 10-11
D-49074 Osnabrück
Tel: (0541) 323 43 15
Fax: (0541) 323 2751
Seats: 639
Class: C
Hotel: Dom Hotel (0541) 358 350

Pforzheim Stadttheater
Am Waisenhausplatz 5
D-75172 Pforzheim
Tel: (07231) 39 28 73
Fax: (07231) 39 14 85
Seats: 510
Class: D
Hotel: Montaner (07231) 10 20 75

Plauen Vogtland Theater
Theaterplatz

D-08523 Plauen
Tel: (03741) 291 24 46
Fax: (03741) 22 26 20
Seats: 467
Class: B
Hotel: Hotel am Theater (03741) 12 10

Theater Regensburg
Bismarkstraße 7
D-93047 Regensburg
Tel: (0941) 507 1425
Fax: (0941) 507 4429
Seats: 528
Class: B
Hotel: Münchener Hof (0941) 58 440

Rostock Volkstheater
Patriotischer Weg 33
D-18057 Rostock
Tel: (0381) 381 0
Fax: (0381) 244 216
Seats: 575
Class: A
Hotel: Gueste Schiff (0381) 49 580

Saarländishes Staatstheater
Schillerplatz 1
D-66111 Saarbrücken
Tel: (0681) 30 92 216
Fax: (0681) 30 92 314
Seats: 875

Class: B
Hotel: Hotel Meran (0681) 653 81

Mecklenburgisches Staatstheater, Schwerin
Alter Garten
D-19055
Tel: (0385) 53 00 122
Fax: (0385)
Seats: 640
Class: A
Hotel: Inter City (0385) 595 00

Stralsund
(see Greifswald)

Staatstheater Stuttgart
Obere Schloßgarten 6
D-70173 Stuttgart
Tel: (0711) 20 32 0
Fax: (0711) 20 32 389
Seats: 1396
Class: A
Hotel: Kronen Hotel (0711) 225 10
      Unger Hotel (0711) 20 990

Trier Stadttheater
Posfach 3470
D-54224 Trier
Tel: (0651) 718 34 64
Fax: (0651) 718 1468
Seats: 622

Class: C
Hotel: Kessler Hotel (0651) 978 170

Ulmer Theater
Olgastraße 73
D-89073 Ulm (Donau)
Tel: (0731) 161 44 34
Fax: (0731) 161 1619
Seats: 815
Class: C
Hotel: Hotel Imbis Ulm (0731) 964 70

Deutsches National Theater Weimar
Theaterplatz 2
Tel: (03643) 755 271
Fax: (03643) 755 307
Seats: 859
Class: A
Hotel: Intercity (03643) 7740

Hessisches Staatstheater
Christian-Zais-Straße 3
D-65189 Wiesbaden
Tel: (0611) 132 266
Fax: (0611) 132 337
Seats: 1041
Class: A
Hotel: Fürstenhof (0611) 52 20 91

Wittenberg Mitteldeutsches Landestheater
Thomas-Münster-Straße 14/15
D-06886 Wittenberg

Tel: (03491) 473 70
Fax: (03491) 473 710
Seats: 388
Class: B
Hotel: Pension an der Stadthalle (03491) 40 40 50

Würzburg Stadttheater
Theaterstraße 21
D-97070 Würzburg
Tel: (0931) 39 08 154
Fax: (0931) 39 08 100
Seats: 756
Class: B
Hotel: Goldene Faß (0931) 321 560

Wuppertal Opernhaus
(also Gelsenkirchen)
Spinnstraße 4
D-42283 Wuppertal
Tel: (0202) 563 42 30
Fax: (0202)
Seats: 836
Class: A
Hotel: Hotel zur Krone (0202) 59 50 20

Theater Zwickau GmbH
Neuberinplatz
D-08056 Zwickau
Tel: (0375) 83 46 00
Fax: (0375) 83 46 09
Seats: 400

Class: B
Hotel: Holiday Inn (0375) 279 20

***

Theaters in Austria

(country code-41)

Stadttheater Baden
Theaterplatz 7
A-2500 Baden bei Wien
Tel: (02252) 4 83 38
Fax: (02252) 4 83 38 40
Seats: 702
Hotel: Park Hotel (02252) 443 86

Graz Opernhaus
Kaiser-Josef-Platz 10
A-8010 Graz
Tel: (0316) 80 08 0
Fax: (0316) 80 08 92
Seats: 1224
Hotel: Gollner (0316) 82 25 21

Tiroler Landestheater
Rennweg 2
A-6020 Innsbrück
Tel: (0512) 5 20 74
Fax: (0512) 5 20 74 333
Seats: 801
Hotel: Graue Bär (0512) 59 24

Klagenfurt Stadttheater
Theaterplatz 4
A-9020 Klagenfurt
Tel: (0463) 5 52 66
Fax: (0463) 5 40 64
Seats: 735
Hotel: Carinthia (0463) 51 16 45

Linz Landestheater
Promenade 39
A-4020 Linz
Tel: (0732) 76 11 0
Fax: (0732) 76 11 308
Seats: 756
Hotel: Hotel zur drei Mohen (0732) 65 26 21

Landestheater Salzburg
Schwarzstraße 22
A-5020 Salzburg
Tel: (0662) 87 15 12 0
Fax: (0662) 87 15 12
Seats: 707
Hotel: Theater Bräu (0662) 889 65

Theater der Landeshauptstadt
Rathausplatz 11
A-3100 St. Pölten
Tel: (02742) 35 20 26
Fax: (02742)35 20 26 52
Seats: 383
Hotel: Hotel Metropol (02742) 786 37

Staatstheater Wien
Opernring 2
A-1010 Wien
Tel: (01) 514 44 0
Fax: (01) 514 44 23 30
Seats: 1709
Hotel: Pension Pertchi (01) 53 44 49
    Roten Hotel (01) 214 3507

Volksoper Wien Gmbh
Währinger Straße 78
A-1090 Wien
Tel: (01) 514 44 30
Fax: (01) 514 44 32 15
Seats: 1313
Hotel: Pension Pertchi (01) 53 44 49
    Roten Hotel (01) 214 3507

***

German-Speaking Theaters in Switzerland
(country code-41)

Stadttheater Basel
Elisabethstraße 16
CH- 4051 Basel
Tel: (061) 295 1100
Fax: (061) 295 1200
Seats: 1115
Hotel: Viktoria (061) 270 70 70

Stadttheater Bern
Nägeligasse 1
CH-3000 Bern
Tel: (031) 329 5111
Fax: (031) 311 3947
Hotel: Hotel Metropol (031) 311 50 21

Stadttheater Biel
Burgasse 13
CH-2500
Tel: (032) 328 89 69
Fax: (032) 22 16 14
Seats: 260
Hotel: Dufour (032) 344 78 78

Stadttheater Luzern
Theaterstraße 2
CH-6002 Luzern
Tel: (041) 210 33 63
Fax: (041) 210 33 67
Seats: 555
Hotel: Hotel Flora (041) 229 79 79
       Hotel des Balances (041) 410 30 10

Stadttheater St. Gallen
Museumstraße 1/24
CH-9004 St. Gallen
Tel: (071) 24 20 511
Fax: (071) 26 05 06
Seats: 741
Hotel: Extra Blatt (071) 223 4503

Opernhaus Zürich
Falkenstraße 1
CH-8008 Zürich
Tel: (01) 268 64 00
Fax: (01) 2 68 64 01
Seats: 1200
Hotel: Ambassador (01) 261 76 00
    See Garten (01) 383 37 37

***

German-Speaking Operetta and Musical Theaters

Theater des Westens
Kantstraße 12
10623 Berlin
Phone: (030)-31 90 30
Fax: (030) 31 90 31 90
website: www.theater-des-westens.de
e-Mail: info@theater-des-westens.de
Hotel: Pension Kettler (030) 883 4949

Musical Theater Berlin
Hunchback of Notre Dame
(Der Glöckner)
Marlene-Dietrich-Platz 1
10785 Berlin
Phone: (030) 2 59 29 0
Fax: (030) 2 59 29 1 10
Hotel: Pension Kettler (030) 883 4949

Theater Bochum
Starlight Express

Stationring 24
44791 Bochum
Phone: (0234) 50 60 20
Hotel: Novotel (0234) 50 640

Neue Metropol Bremen Theater
Produktion GmbH & Co.
Jeckyll & Hyde
Grünenweg 5-7
28195 Bremen
Phone: (0421) 3 33 77
Fax: (0421) 3 33 75 55
Hotel: Lichtsinn am Park (0421) 368 070

Staatsoperette Dresden
Pirnaer Landstr. 131
01257 Dresden
Phone: (0351) 2 07 99 0
Fax: (0351) 2 07 99 22
Hotel: Kampinski Hotel

Düsseldorfer Operette e.V.
Schlesische Str. 94
40231 Düsseldorf
Phone: (0211) 22 22 81
Fax: (0211) 71 50 43
Hotel: (0211) 323 06 21

Operettenhaus Hamburg
Cats
Spielbudenplatz 1
20359 Hamburg

Phone: (040) 31 11 70
Hotel: Hotel am Rothenbaum (040) 446 006

Neue Flora
Phantom der Oper
Stresemannstr. 159a
22769 Hamburg
Phone: (040) 43 16 50
Hotel: Pension Fink (040) 44 05 71

BUDDY Musicaltheater
The Buddy Holly Story
Norderelbstr. 6
20475 Hamburg
Phone: (040) 31 78 07-0
Fax: (040) 31 78 07-10
Hotel: Pension Rode (040) 44 28 75

Oper Leipzig Musicalische Komödie
Dreilindenstr. 30
04177 Leipzig
Phone: (0341) 12 61 19
Fax: (0341) 1 26 11 50
Hotel: Hotel (0341) 12 61 130

Die Schöne und das Biest Theater
Plieninger Str. 109
70567 Stuttgart
Phone: (0711) 9 00 66 0
Fax: (0711) 900 66 6 10
Hotel:Kronen Hotel (0711) 225 10
        Unger Hotel (0711) 20 990

PART TWO

Auditioning in the German-Speaking Countries

"If you really want to sing, and singing to me means communicating, you must learn the language you want to sing in. Germany and Italy are a must, but don't think that 6 months will do it. To sing properly you must absorb a nation's culture. Never speak or think in English. Don't give up hope and be grateful for every chance you get to sing. Take every opportunity and do not think of a career, think of life and enjoy every minute. Europe is so wonderful! You will never be bored, and with a bit of luck and perseverance, everything will fall into place."

John Dew, Stage Director and Designer

Chapter Seven

"How Much is this Going to cost me?"

Without a doubt, one of your greatest concerns throughout this auditioning experience will be how much it all will cost in terms of dollars. Very few singers have unlimited resources, and therefore need to watch every penny. We discuss in other chapters how one can save money. Here are actual costs (as of this writing) one can incur while traveling throughout the German-speaking countries. We hope this will give you at least an idea of how much you will need to budget for your upcoming audition tour. Let us assume you will be staying for 60 days, and have at least ten auditions scheduled during that time.

A note about payment:

Since the rate of exchange fluctuates every day, it is our opinion that you should always use your American credit card (MasterCard, Visa, and American Express) whenever possible. Almost everyone accepts them now, and you will not have to be worrying all the time about losing cash. But the main reason is *you will save an enormous amount of money using credit cards instead of exchanging cash.* Let us explain.

As of this writing the dollar is trading at 2DM. However, in reality, when you go to the bank to trade your greenbacks for *Marks*, you will receive only about 1.94DM for each dollar. If that is not painful enough, when you return to the bank to exchange your *Marks* for dollars, you will have to pay about 2.06DM for each dollar. You lose either way. However, when you use your American credit card, you pay exactly what the rate of exchange is for that day. Some credit cards do, however, charge a 1 percent fee for payment in foreign currency. So call and ask. Nevertheless, it is still cheaper to use your credit card.

Also, ask your credit/debit card company to provide you with a PIN number. That way you will have no trouble withdrawing cash.

We do recommend bringing at least $200-$400 in cash or travelers cheques just in case you encounter unforeseen trouble with your credit card.

The following are some figures you may use as a guideline. We have purposely calculated costs on the high side.

Round-trip plane ticket from the States-$500

Eurail Pass- 15 consecutive days   -$554
             21 consecutive days   -$718
             1 month   -$890
             2 months   -$1,260

Paß der Deutschen Bahn (2nd Class)   -5 days (within one month)-
                                       $196
                                       -10 days (within one month)-
                                       $306*

Hotel-$50-$60 per day (100-120DM) X 60 = $3,000-$3,600

Food-$20 per day (35DM) X 60 = $1,200

Telephone (*Handy*)-$100 (200DM)

Telephone Calls-$10 per day X 60 = $600

Coaches/Accompanists-$20 X 15 = $300

Bahncard-$130 (260DM for one year, which reduces each train ticket by half) *

Bahn Travel-10 X 120DM ($60) = $600 (when using the *Bahncard*)

Misc.-$20 X 60 = $1200
(postage, snacks, toiletries, gifts, etc..)

* One or the other, not necessarily both.

Grand Total: $8,000-$9,000

***

We told you that it was going to be on the high side. Obviously, most if not all of you are going to stay with friends some of the time, which will greatly reduce your hotel costs. As we will discuss in another chapter, finding a small apartment will also reduce your hotel and food expenditures as well. In fact, we believe you can cut those costs in half, as two of our friends did by making plans early. Below are the budgets of two singers, one female (singer A) and one male (singer B), who both did audition tours in the Fall/Winter of 1999. Singer A came from California. Singer B came from New York.

***

Singer A

Before leaving the States, Singer A raised nearly $10,000 through gifts, proceeds from recitals, and from her own savings. She was in Germany and Switzerland for a total of nine weeks. For her first month, she bought a ten-day German Rail Pass. When she extended her stay for the second month, she bought a one-month Eurail Pass. During most of her audition tour, she stayed with friends, who not only housed her, but fed her as well. Needless to say, her friends saved her quite a bit of money. Excluding any pre-tour preparations, her expenses were as follows:

Transportation-$2,150

Phone/Fax Expenses-$685

Housing-$320

Food-$350

Post-$150

Internet Cafés-$115

Misc.-$1,200 (approximate)

Total: $5,000 (approximate)

✱✱✱

Singer B

Singer B's audition tour lasted approximately eight weeks. His preparation and continued housing expenses in the States totaled nearly $4,500. He found a furnished apartment for his "home base" in Germany that cost $600 per month. He therefore saved money on food as well by preparing most of his meals there. These were his expenses excluding pre-tour preparation:

Transportation-$1,000

Housing-$1,200

Food-$800

Misc.-$500

Total: $3,500 (approximate)

Chapter Eight

Using the Telephone in Europe

What follows is very basic information; nevertheless, we feel that it is very important information that everyone should know. There is nothing more frustrating than being in Germany or one of the other German-speaking countries, hearing about an audition, or just wanting to call home, and not knowing for sure what numbers to dial.

Calling from the U.S.:

Note that all area codes in European cities are preceded by "0." When calling from the U.S., dial "011" to get outside the States, then the appropriate country code (Germany "49"; Switzerland "41"; Austria "43"), then drop the "0" before the area code, followed by the area code and number you wish to dial. For example, to fax something *from* America *to* the *ZBF* Agency in Berlin ("030" is the area code for Berlin), dial the following:

011 49 30 757 60 249

***

Calling within Germany:

While in Germany, calling from city to city, simply dial "0" plus the area code and number. For example, let's say you are staying with a friend in Hamburg and you want to fax your resumé to the *ZBF* in Berlin. Dial the following:

030 757 60 249

***

Calling from the German-speaking countries to the U.S.:

To the U.S., dial "001" plus the area code and number.

***

Calling between the European countries:

Between European countries, simply dial "00" then the corresponding country code, then drop the "0" before the area code, followed by the area code and number. For example, you are in Austria, and you have to fax your resumé to the *ZBF* in Berlin. Dial the following:

00 49 30 757 60 249

***

Telephone costs:

Using the telephone in Germany in the past has been outrageously expensive. However, the 1998 deregulation of the telecommunication companies throughout the European Community has drastically brought down prices. In 1992, we paid 3.20DM (about $2 at that time) *per minute* calling to the States. Now, from a home phone, it can be as low as 12 *Pfennige* (about 6') per minute.

***

Mobile Telephones:

It is our recommendation that the second you arrive in Europe (specifically Germany) you should purchase a mobile phone (in Germany, referred to as a *"Handy"*) from D-2, D-1, or E-PLUS. As of this writing, the cost for one year, including the phone (which you get to keep), reloadable calling card, and voice-mailbox is only 199DM (about $100). With it, you receive 50DM worth of calls, *and* (are you ready for this?) *you pay nothing to receive calls.* When will we ever catch on to this one in the States?

It is irresponsible for you not to be able to be reached as soon as you arrive abroad. So go straight to one of the phone companies we mentioned and sign up. Whenever you arrive, just ask where the nearest office of one of the companies we mentioned is located. They seem to be on every street corner.

***

Pre-Paid Telephone Calling-Cards:

Even before you pick up your *Handy*, go to the *Post* (post office) and buy a calling card. They may be purchased for either 12DM and 50DM. *Important*: If you buy a 50DM card, you actually get 60DM worth of calls. As of recently, you can also buy the cards at the *Bahnhof Reise Zentrum* (train station ticket office) and some of the *Tabac* shops. Do not travel without a calling card. Sometimes there are no coin-phones to be found.

***

Coin Pay-Phones:

They do exist, but not everywhere. Sometimes they do come in handy, but please, take our advice and *always* have a pre-paid German phone-card in your pocket.

Chapter Nine

Audition Wardrobe

This is the fun part. Here is what we have observed. The best advice we can share is this: Wear what looks good on you and what makes you feel comfortable. For women, this includes pantsuits, a longish skirt and nice blouse or a dress. And men, you will be so glad to know that you can get a job even if you are just wearing a nice pair of slacks and a turtleneck at your audition. This applies to conductors and accompanists as well. We have seen this happen with our own eyes. As a matter of fact, I (William) have not worn a jacket for the past three years at auditions. So let good taste, freedom of movement, and good grooming take the place of insanely expensive three-piece suits and your knock-off little Chanel numbers. You really do not have to go overboard here.

Now, having said that, if you feel your best in a three-piece suit, guys, then that is what you should wear. Ladies, if you feel that you will sing your very best in stiletto heels and a mini skirt, then go for it. But if you look just as good in something more relaxed, that is perfectly acceptable at auditions, even at larger house auditions. Don't be shocked. This is how things are in Germany. We have been at auditions where we have seen ladies bring out full-length evening gowns. This has only caused the giggles for the folks listening. Good taste is *always* the rule of thumb.

Chapter Ten

Transportation

Okay, this can get complicated, but since we are people who really do not thrive on complications, we will cut to the quick of things: *Take the train.* Period.

We are assuming that as you read, you will already have purchased your plane ticket, and that what you are looking at here is the very real concern about getting from the airport to your new digs, then to your appointed auditions. So relax and continue reading. You are going to get advice "straight from the horse's mouth."

Rest assured that each and every town to which you may need to travel, will indeed have both a train stop and a taxi service. Taxis can be a big help, so be sure to keep cash on hand. Keep in mind, one cannot just flag down a taxi like we do in New York. You will either have to go to a *Taxi Stand*, always located at the train station and other congested areas of the city, or you will have to telephone one. The *Deutsche Bahn* provides a service in which the train conductor will call and make sure a taxi is waiting for you at your destination. This service will cost you about 5DM. Otherwise, as soon as you arrive at your destination, go to the nearest *Telefonzelle* (phone booth), look on the cover of the phone book or on the wall of the phone booth itself, and voilá, there you will find the number for the local taxi service.

Your best bet if you are an absolute first-time traveler over here is to purchase a Eurailpass through an American travel service before you come. It's a little more expensive, but as we said, if it's your first time over, it's worth the convenience if you can afford it. This pass will give you the flexibility to travel anywhere you need to go, at anytime of any given day. With it you will also have the great honor of getting to ride in the First Class sections of trains, which can be rather relaxing if you have a long day's travel in store. The other benefit of the Eurailpass is that if you are at all unsure of your German language skills, you will not have to go into the *Reisezentrum* (ticket office) to buy a ticket for upcoming trips.

Now, should you be a seasoned traveler, with lots of courage and bravado, you may want to buy a *Bahncard*. This is a discount-card the train service offers here, in which all of your tickets, wherever you are traveling, will cost you 50% of the regular fare. The price of the *Bahncard* is 260DM ($130), and it is good for one year, and can be purchased at any German train station. That way you will have it next year when you begin your new job! This is a rather neat idea, but something we really suggest for a more experienced traveler, just because of the exercise of having to buy tickets separately for each of your auditions. However, if you think you can stand in line at the train station without feeling any stress about it, then this is really the best use of your money.

Important: Make sure you always have a few spare passport-size photos with you. They will require one for the *Bahncard* when applying. It will appear on the face of the card.

Another option is a *Paß der Deutschen Bahn* (German-rail pass). This pass is issued as a first- or second-class ticket with five or ten days of travel within a 30-day period. It is not terribly expensive, and you will have no problem getting where you need to go within Germany.

However, should you have business outside of Deutschland, the Eurailpass is the better choice.

As you can see, there are a number of options available, and most reputable American travel agencies will supply the latest information on these train-travel options, since, like everything else, their options and prices are subject to change. Ask them. Just walk into an office, and ask an agent if German rail passes are available. If they say, "The German what?" find another travel agent. You may now also buy both the German- and Eurailpasses in Germany as well as in the States. Right now, the best Website to turn to is *www.der.com/Rail.*

There is also a Website address for the *Deutsche Bahn* (German rail system) with some valuable information in English as well as in German. The Website is *www.bahn.de.*

Below are the prices (as of January, 2000) for the Eurail and German rail passes, as well as a list of train stations where they may be purchased:

Eurail Pass-	15 consecutive days	-$554
	21 consecutive days	-$718
	1 month	-$890
	2 months	-$1,260

In Germany, the Eurail Pass may be purchased only at the following train stations:

Berlin Zoo	*Heidelberg Hbf*
Dresden Hbf	*Köln Hbf*
Frankfurt Hbf	*Leipzig Hbf*

Frankfurt Flughafen   *München Hbf*
Hamburg Hbf   *Stuttgart Hbf*
Hannover Hbf

Paß der Deutschen Bahn-2nd Class   -5 days (within one month)-
                                        $196
                                        -10 days (within one month)-
                                        $306*

In addition to the stations listed above, the German Rail Pass may also be purchased at the following train stations:

Basel Bad Bf
Berlin Schönefeld Flughafen
Düsseldorf Hbf
Düsseldorf Flughafen
München Flughafen

Something that might be a good idea to keep in mind about trains: They are a great and convenient way to travel. You can sleep on them (which, as we said earlier, we don't recommend unless absolutely necessary), use your laptops, and even get decaf on those great, noble, fast time-tested vehicles. What we want to emphasize here is this: The train is a relaxing, reliable way to get to where you need to be. They accept Visa, Mastercard, and cash. They are even equipped with telephones. You can buy a telephone card from the *Schaffner* (conductor) for a mere 12DM ($6.00) in case you forgot to pick-up one at the *Post*.

If for some reason you have missed your scheduled train, do not fret. There is almost always a train at least one or two hours later. Simply walk over to the posted train schedule. (The *departure* schedule is a large, *bright-yellow* poster, usually in a glass case, located on every train platform. The *arrival* schedule is *white*.) Your next step should be to grab your *Handy* (cell phone), put in a call to the theater or agent where you have a scheduled audition, to let them know that you missed your train, and ask if you can arrive late. If they say no, then ask them if there is another audition date that you could attend. The most important thing is to keep your cool, and *always call if you are going to be late or miss an audition.*

Remember, deciding to buy a Eurail Pass, German Pass, or a *Bahncard* depends on your individual schedule and personal needs. So think this through carefully.

Chapter Eleven

Accommodations While Auditioning

Without a doubt, the best way to reduce your expenditures significantly while auditioning is to find a small apartment and use it as your "home base." They are not easy to find, but they are out there. Staying with friends for a couple of days is great, but don't do it for weeks at a time. Your friends will have their own stresses with rehearsals, learning music, etc. They will need their privacy, and so do you. Besides, you will be more concentrated on what you have come to accomplish: getting a job. And believe us, your auditions will go better if you have your "own" place.

You should be able to find a furnished efficiency or one-bedroom apartment for $400-$600 a month, and sometimes even less. (Think of the savings. A hotel would cost you at least $1,500 a month for a room the size of a closet.) The advantages are endless. You will have a home base. You will have a kitchen that will save you a fortune compared with going out to eat every day. Mail takes only one day in Germany, so agents can contact you by post if for some reason you can't be reached on the Handy you picked up when you arrived. Please, if there is one piece of advice that you glean from this chapter, let it be this: *Get your own place.*

How to find a short-term apartment:

As we said earlier, these places are not easy to find if you are in the States. The word is finally getting out to those Americans singing over here who travel frequently and have empty apartments for weeks at a time. Some have actually advertised on www.ClassicalSinger.com. So look there first. You should also put a "wanted" ad on the same Web site as well.

Next, contact *every* person you know living in Europe. Ask them if they know about a place. Also, if you have a friend working in a theater, send them a *Suche* (wanted) ad and ask them to place it on the bulletin board there.

Another possibility would be to go to www.yahoo.de, then search under *Zeitungen* (newspapers) or *kleine Zeitungen* (small newspapers) for newspapers in the specific area where you want to stay. Then search for *Wohnungen* (apartments). This is sort of new, but it's worth a try.

"Der Sänger muß bemüht sein, Resonanz und Stütze immer in gleichformigen Zusammenhang für den Klang des Tones zu bekommen. Alle Übungen müssen dort so sein, daß die Stimme ohne Drück ver-grössern und arbeiten kann."

("The singer should always strive to combine the elements of support and resonance in the interest of vocal quality. Every exercise must open the way for the voice to function and amplify itself without being forced in any way.")

Marianne Fischer-Kupfer
Komische Oper Berlin

Chapter Twelve

The Audition Experience

You have spent years and countless dollars preparing for this audition-ing experience, so do everything within your power to protect your audition days. Having said that, accept the fact that some things are out of your control. Of course, you cannot control the weather, nor the punctuality of the trains and taxis. Sometimes you cannot control how much sleep you get the night before your audition, nor how your body and throat feel on a particular day. Getting past all this is what separates the professional singer from the amateur.

There are certain things you do have control over. You obviously do not go out the night before and drink a keg of Germany's finest. Do that after you get the job. Nor do you stay up all night talking to your American colleagues, even if you haven't seen them for ten years. Again, *you are here to get a job.* You can visit afterwards. Also, try your best to avoid restaurants. You won't believe how smoky they can be.

***

Confirm Your Audition

Whatever you do, *call a day or two before the audition* to make sure it is still taking place. Even if an agent has set up a house audition for you, *you* should call the *Künstlerisches Betriebsbüro* (the artistic administra-tion office), or *KBB*, directly and make sure you are scheduled to sing. We are all human, and even agents make mistakes, as do the theaters. I (William) have actually had two agents send me to auditions where the theater specifically told them they only wanted to hear tenors, and didn't need any baritones. Twice this happened. It cost me a lot of money, and looking back, I should have insisted on being reimbursed by the agents. They, of course, pleaded ignorance.

***

Rental Cars

There are some other things that might not be so obvious. We realize this may sound a bit dogmatic, but we are going to say it anyway. *Never, ever drive a car to an audition.* Don't even let a friend drive you, unless it is only a few kilometers away, and we mean ten or twenty. We have owned cars in Germany and have driven everywhere there is to drive: in the East, in the West, in the country, in the city, even to Czechoslovakia. So we know what we are talking about. All we ever hear from our colleagues who drive is *Stau* (traffic jam) this and *Stau* that. *Anything* can happen on the Autobahn at *any time*. The train is still the *safest* and most dependable mode of transportation. And ultimately, you will save no money driving, paying $4 a gallon for gasoline.

***

Night Trains

The other thing that we discourage, though we are constantly amazed at those auditionees who insist on doing it, is taking the night-train at *any time* during your audition tour. Yes, it's safe. That's not the point. But why expose your body to that sort of fatigue that will only make you more vulnerable to getting sick? And all that, to save $50-$60 on a hotel! The last thing you need during your audition tour is the flu or even a cold. Taking care of your body and voice is the most important thing you can do while traveling. That also means getting as much rest as possible, which brings us to our next point.

***

The Day Before

Forget about getting to an audition an hour before. *When possible,* we recommend getting there *the day before, especially* if it is a house audition. We realize this may not always be possible. However, when it is, *do it.* That way, you can acclimate yourself to the city and the agent's office or the theater. If it's a house audition, go to the theater the day before and introduce yourself to the *Pförtner* (the door man/porter). He will be glad to give you a key to one of the practice rooms (if they all aren't already taken), and if you are lucky, you may be able to sneak on the stage and sing a few notes. Keep in mind that most rehearsals take place from 10.00 until 14.00 and again from 18.00 until 22.00. (Yes, Europe uses the 24-hour clock, so learn it now.) Oftentimes, in the afternoon there is absolutely no one on the stage, so take advantage of that. In addition, when possible, try to find out who will be playing for the audition. If you are singing something like Zerbinetta's aria, the accompanist will appreciate knowing about it beforehand.

A note of advice: We realize that it is not always possible, but at least try to avoid scheduling auditions too closely together, especially if they are on opposite ends of the country.

***

The Day of Your Vorsingtermin

Auditioning for Agents

On the day of the audition, you obviously will need to be there at least an hour before, whether it be an agent or a house audition. If you see old friends, say hello and meet with them *after* the audition. *Stay focused on what you came to accomplish.* If you are singing for an agent, you will not get to rehearse with the accompanist. We are not trying to be negative here, but do not expect to encounter the same quality of pianists that play at New York auditions. Many times an agent will invite a student to play an audition who has never played any of the operatic repertoire, much less yours. Often the accompanist playing for those auditioning is being auditioned himself. (Doesn't that bring you comfort?) We have actually had pianists tell us they simply cannot play what we have put in front of them. Some have even stopped playing while we were singing. If that is not enough, they still expect us to pay them. Unfortunately, there is no getting out of that one, as the agents do not pay the accompanists. The auditionees do. So be prepared to pay them 20-30DM, no matter how they play.

***

Theater Auditions

When you arrive at the theater, check-in immediately with the *Pförtner*. He will usually have your name on the auditionee list. He will either refer you to the *KBB* or the *Korrepetitor* (accompanist). Again, make sure you arrive ahead of time (at least an hour). This way you can get a practice room, and you will not feel so rushed. You will also have general-information forms to fill out (education, repertoire, nationality, etc.), so don't forget your German/English dictionary.

We wish we could tell you that when you go to a theater audition, the pianists there will be much better. Unfortunately, this too varies greatly. One day you may have the best pianist you could ever imagine, and on the next you will want to ask the accompanist to get off the bench so you can play yourself. (I actually met someone who did this.) This is where we will unapologetically say that American accompanists far surpass their German counterparts. We have yet to figure out why. There are certainly a number of excellent pianists in Germany. Maybe it's because there are many more performing opportunities for pianists here in Europe than there are in the States, and the good ones would rather be performing rather than just accompanying auditions or rehearsals. Who knows? Nevertheless, be prepared not to get the quality you would normally get at home.

Unlike the agent audition, you will generally have the opportunity to work with your accompanist before the audition when you sing for a theater. You are not expected to pay them as you do the agent accompanists; however, if they play exceptionally well, it wouldn't hurt to tip them 10DM.

**

A word about printed music

Do not use laminated music. This is a specific request from accompanists with whom we have met. The light varies from stage to stage, and sometimes it is hard enough for the pianist to see. The reflection from the plastic makes it that much more difficult, if not impossible. Also, *clearly* mark *every* fermata, tempo change, cuts, etc. We know you have heard all this before, but for some reason singers continue to come to auditions with unacceptable copies of music and still expect miracles from the accompanists. Remember, this is *your* audition—which brings us to our next point.

**

Introducing Yourself

Your audition begins the second you walk through the door. That goes for pianists, conductors, and singers as well. How you present yourself, before you even open your mouth, can make all the difference in the world.

At both the agent and theater auditions, always try to speak as much German as possible. If you say anything, say, *"Guten Tag! Mein Name ist Jane Doe. Ich komme aus New York, und möchte mit Gilda's Aria anfangen."* ("Hello, my name is Jane Doe. I am from New York, and would like to begin with Gilda's aria.") They will often ask, *"Was haben Sie noch?"* ("What else can you offer us?"), to which you reply, *"Ich habe auch Musetta, Manon, und Glitter and be Gay mitgebracht."* ("I have also brought Musetta, Manon, and Glitter and be Gay.") If they want to hear a second aria, you can almost count on hearing, *"Haben Sie was auf deutsch?"* ("Do you have something in German?").

This will sound extremely cold, but if you do not have anything to sing for them in German, *then stay at home until you do.* This is Germany, and even in some of the "A" houses *The Marriage of Figaro* is sung in German, not to mention the numerous other operas whose original text is not in German.

If they say a loud *"Danke!"* after you sing, that means you are basically finished. *It does not necessarily mean they are not interested in you.* They may have twenty-five more sopranos to listen to that day. Simply be polite and say, *"Vielen Dank! Aufwiedersehen!"* ("Thank you very much. Until next time.") If you have the time, and there are not a lot of people auditioning, stay around after the audition. If the people who just listened to you see you afterwards, and they liked you, they will more than likely give you some feedback. This can always be helpful. Some theaters actually call every auditionee into their office after the audition, whether they are interested in hiring you or not. This information can be invaluable to your future auditions and singing in general. So hang around.

To emphasize the importance of language, as we have in an earlier chapter, we relate to you a story recently shared with us by one of our conductor friends:

A tenor came to sing an audition in a theater. He gracefully walked on stage and in perfect German introduced himself, *"Guten Tag! Ich heiße John Doe. Ich möchte für Sie Taminos Aria vorsingen."* ("Hello! My name is John Doe. I would like to sing Tamino's aria for you.") The theater staff immediately replied, *"Guten Tag, Herr Doe! Was haben Sie noch?"* ("Hello, Mr. Doe. What else do you have?") to which he replied, *"Guten Tag! Ich heiße John Doe. Ich möchte für Sie Taminos Aria vorsingen."*

So, learn the language!

PART THREE

"Now that I have a job..."

Chapter Thirteen

Housing in Germany
(after you have your job)

One would think that after having lived here for nine years, and having been engaged in three different theaters, we would have some well-kept secrets to share with you on how one goes about locating that "dream apartment" once you begin your job. Sorry, it's not that easy. At the same time, it isn't that complicated. So, hang in there, be patient, and use all resources available.

The first thing you need to do is to tell the *KBB* that you need a place to live. Sometimes they will help you, sometimes they won't. If they don't, then put up a *"Suche"* (Wanted) ad on the bulletin board at the theater. Try to do this by May or June, and plan to move into your new apartment at least one week before you have to begin rehearsals. That way you have plenty of time to get melded, pick-up your visa, etc. We will discuss these things in the next chapter. Since you will likely be in the States in the spring, send a fax to your *KBB*, and insist, nicely, that they post your "Apartment Wanted" ad for you. If you get no response within a couple of weeks try to get someone to send you a copy of the apartment ads in the local newspaper. Something new, but certain to become extremely helpful in the near future, are on-line apartment ads. Go to www.yahoo.de, search for local *Zeitungen* (newspapers), and follow links to *Wohnungen* (apartments).

The problem we often find in Germany is that one has to give two to three months notice before moving out of their apartment. So, timing on your part is important here. If you realize that you are going to get off the plane with no place to live, please make sure that the *KBB* knows this. Ask them where they house their guests who come for extended stays. Though it might cost you a little extra money, it will give you piece of mind, and the opportunity to actually see the apartment you will be considering before you sign a rental agreement. It varies greatly, but since your funds will be limited, try to get the *Vermieter* (landlord) to charge you only one month *Kaution* (deposit). Make sure you are clear as to whether the *Miete* (rent) is *Kaltmiete* (not including heat) or *Warmiete* (including heat). Also make sure you are clear as to what other utilities you are expected to pay.

Expect to purchase *all* your appliances, including the kitchen sink (we are not joking!), unless you find a former employee of the theater who just happens not to be taking those items with them to their next apartment. It is acceptable for them to expect payment from you up front for these items, and sometimes for the light fixtures as well.

Ruhestunde (quiet hours)—yes, it really is true. There are quiet hours in Germany. In general, your neighbor should not hear you between noon or 13.00, depending on where you live, and 15.00, nor after 20.00, and definitely not after 22.00.

Chapter Fourteen

Regeln, Regeln, Regeln!
(Rules, Rules, Rules!)

It will seem to most Americans that Germans are obsessed with rules and doing things the "right" way. Get used to it and learn to deal with it the best you can. After all, it is their system that provides an unbelievable opportunity for opera singers and other artists.

Here are some logistical things you are required to do by law if you are going to live and work there. Some of these things change from year to year, so do your best to make sure you are up-to-date with them. Ask the administration in the theater and your colleagues as well. Remember, ultimately *you* are responsible for making sure they get done, not the theater. Americans civilians living in Germany can attest to how frustrating and time consuming all this can be. We hope the following information will at least prepare you for what one can expect.

IMPORTANT: As a rule, when taking care of the following procedures, it will save you a lot of time and heartache if you bring these items along:

1. Passports (yours and your family members', if they are traveling with you)

2. Your contract from the theater

3. Your rental contract from your landlord, if you have one. If you do not, or you are an *Untermieter* (sublessor), have whomever you are

renting from sign the *Mietbescheinigung/Bestätigung* (rent certifi-
cate/confirmation) that you will pick up from the
Einwohnermelderamt (residence registration office).

4. *Cash* to pay for certain fees (100DM for your *Aufenthalterlaubnis*
   and 50DM for each dependent as of this writing)

5. Your *Arbeitserlaubnis* (work permit), when you have it

6. Your *Aufenthalterlaubnis* (visa), when you have it

7. A very long book and/or Game Boy. The wait at the various agencies
   can be painfully long.

***

Work Permits and Visas

As soon as you receive a *Vertrag* (contract) you must apply for an
Aufenthalterlaubnis (visa). If you are in the States, contact your nearest
German consulate. If there is enough time, usually about eight weeks, you
can actually take care of this before you return to Germany. Otherwise,
you will have to do it in Germany before you begin your job. Some theaters will do this for you without your asking. Some will not. Make sure
you ask. If you have to do it yourself, you will go to the *Ausländerbehörde*
(foreign affairs office), located in or near the *Rathaus*, (city hall) of each
city. You should have an extra passport-size photo with you and, of course,
your passport, your contract from the theater, and at least 100DM. If you
have dependents, you will need the same for each of them.

Note:

Don't be surprised when you go to the visa office, and they say to
you, "Sorry, but we will need your work permit first." No, that's not a
joke. It seems to vary from day to day and from city to city as to which
you need first, the visa, or the work permit. Our recommendation is to
get your visa first, then as soon as possible (the same day, perhaps),

apply for your work permit unless, of course, the theater has already done it for you.

Again, just as with your visa, some theaters will take care of applying for your *Arbeitserlaubnis* (work permit). If not, go to the *Arbeitsamt* (employment office) with your contract and passport, which will have your visa inside. Remember, take a book or your Game Boy with you. It may be a long wait.

It may seem trivial to even mention this, but it is hard for an American to conceive that any government office would be closed in the middle of the day, or have different office hours each day of the week. To add to the confusion, there doesn't seem to be any consistency between government agencies. We hope the following information will help. Remember, the 24-hour clock is used throughout Europe. Also, there is no colon, but a period between the hour and minutes. Here are the office hours of the *Arbeitsamt* and *Ausländerbehörde* where we presently live. They should be similar to those in other German cities as well.

Arbeitsamt Office Hours

Monday	07.30-15.30
Tuesday	07.30-15.30
Wednesday	closed
Thursday	07.30-18.00
Friday	07.30-12.30

Ausländerbehörde Office Hours

Monday	08.00-11.00
Tuesday	08.00-11.00, 13.00-15.00

Wednesday closed
Thursday 08.00-11.00, 13.00-16.30
Friday 08.00-11.00

***

Anmeldung (registering)

When establishing your legal residency in Germany, which you must do if you accept a *Festvertrag*, the first thing you have to do after you find an apartment is register (*anmelden*) with the proper authorities. This you will do with the cities' *Einwohnermelderamt* (The residency registration office. Don't you just love these long words?). The location of the *Einwohnermeldeamt* varies from city to city, so just ask someone in the theater where is is located. Unfortunately, you will probably have to make two trips. You will first pick up a form that your landlord will have to sign, then bring it back to the *Anwohnermelderamt* with a copy of your contract. You must do this within 14 days of moving to a German city or town. When you move to another city, as you move up the ladder in the *fest* system, you will then have to un-register (*abmelden*) from your current address. When you relocate, register (*anmelden*) once again in your new town, following the same procedure.

***

Steuerkarte (tax card)

VERY IMPORTANT: When you are *anmeld*-ing, ask them if you can pick up your *Steuerkarte* or tax card there as well. For some reason, in some cities, you pick this up at the *Arbeitsamt,* and in others at the *Anwohnermelderamt. Without your* Steuerkarte, *you cannot get paid.*

Also, make sure they have the correct *Steuerklasse* (tax bracket) written on your *Steuerkarte* (*Klass 1* if you are single, *Klass 3* if you are married). There is *nothing* more frustrating than being married with three children and finding out you have been taxed as a single person, even if it is for only one month. The difference in take-home pay is considerable.

***

Krankenkasse (health insurance)

When hired, you will be asked to choose a *Krankenversicherung* (health insurance provider). If you are a resident of Germany, you have no choice in this matter. You must be covered. In Germany there is *gesetzliche Versicherung* (state subsidized) and *privat Versicherung* (privately owned). One must earn at least 78,000DM annually to qualify for *privat Versicherung*. Six-thousand DM/per month for a 13-month salary would bump you up into this category. *If you travel back and forth to the United States frequently and earn enough to qualify for this type of policy, it should be considered since you will be covered worldwide with most private policies.*

***

Lifetime Visas and Work Permits

After five consecutive years of living in Germany , one may apply for an *unbefristete Arbeitserlaubnis* (lifetime work permit) and your *unbefristete Aufenthaltserlaubnis* (lifetime visa). You do this at the same locations mentioned above. From then on, when you move from city to city, you simply give the appropriate authorities copies of your permits.

Chapter Fifteen

Theater Pay
(The Rude Awakening)

One of the biggest shocks to Americans singing for the first time in Germany is the net pay, or lack thereof. As of this writing, I (William) have been working non-stop for nearly nine seasons. I am engaged in a Class "A" house in Germany. I do only lead roles, and to my knowledge have never received a "bad" review. My salary is approximately 6,100DM per month. It is greater than the second example given, and less than the third.

All artists are paid for 13 months per year. One-third of the thirteenth month is paid out in June and two-thirds is paid out in November. An additional 500DM is paid out in June as *Urlaubsgeld* (vacation money). It will always be difficult to calculate exactly what this extra pay will be, since it often bumps you up in a higher tax bracket for that month.

The pay examples found in this chapter were provided to me by my friend and *Steuerberater* (tax advisor), Frank Neuhaus. He works for the *KDM Steuerberatungsgesellschaft mbH* in Hannover. (Thank you, Frank!)

Included in these pay examples is the deduction for the *Bayerisher Versorgungskammer (BVK)*, which is required of all artists in the theater. For the *BVK*, 4½ percent of your gross income is added to your pay by the theater and deposited into an account. You will match this by 4½% from your own funds. It is much like an American 401K plan. We will talk more about this "fund" later.

Also included is the *3 percent agent fee.*

Note: German law permits agents to receive a provision of 12 percent from the gross income of a singer's one-year *Festvertrag*. Half (6 percent) is paid by the artist, and half is paid by the theater. The theater may pay the agent directly, while deducting the artist's portion plus sales tax (16 percent based on the entire agent provision). Sometimes the theater simply adds its 6 percent to the artist's income (though it is not taxable), and it is then the responsibility of the artist to pay the agent directly. Since most initial *Festverträge* are for two years, the agent fee is spread out over that period, thus splitting 6percent over two years instead of 12 percent over one.

Now, if *ZBF* sends you to audition in a theater, the theater pays them 3 percent. *Basta!* However, if a private agent like Ocklenburg sends you to audition, you will pay them 3 percent and the theater will pay them 3 percent. In addition to that (and don't ask us why!) you will pay a 16 percent sales tax to the agent, based on the entire 6 percent. For example, let's say your monthly salary is 5000DM:

5000DM Gross pay
x 6% Agent Deduction
300DM (You actually pay only half of this. The other half of this amount is added to your pay by the theater.)

300DM Agent fee
x 16% (Sales tax. Yes, sales tax.)
48DM

300DM
+ *48DM*
348DM Total amount to agent
-*150DM* The amount the theater pays
192DM, or in reality about 4% of your gross salary. (The total amount you actually pay.)

A word about *Freibeträge* (tax deductions): As mentioned earlier, take as many deductions as you legally can, just as you would in the States. Unfortunately, as of January 1, 2000 there is no longer the flat annual *Künstlerfreibetrag* (artist deduction). However, you still may deduct voice lessons, travel, etc. Just make sure you keep your receipts. Whatever you do, hire a good *Steuerberater* (tax advisor) to do your taxes. (We have already mentioned one. They are not allowed to advertise in Germany, so that's all we will say.) They can advise you on what you can and cannot deduct. If, for example, you are supporting family members outside the country, this is a *major* deduction. If your *Steuerberater* says it isn't, get a new *Steuerberater*!

A word about *Kirchensteuer* (church tax): It will be deducted only if you are a member of a German-registered church (i.e. Roman Catholic or Protestant). If you do not want to pay this tax, which can add up over the years, you *must* put "*Freikirche*" on your *Steuerkarte*; otherwise, you will be forced to pay the tax. This deduction *is* included on the following examples.

The standard deductions are:

Lohnsteuer-income tax

Kirchensteuer-church tax

Solidaritätszuschlag (SolZ)-a politically correct term meaning: "money taken from your salary to help rebuild the former East Germany."

Krankenversicherung/Pflegeversicherung (KV/PV)-health insurance/invalid care (Half of this is paid by the theater, and the other half by you. The rates vary from 11.9 percent to 14 percent for the entire amount.)

Rentenversicherung (RV)-retirement pension

Altersversorge (AV)-old age pension (Don't ask us the difference between the *RV* and *AV*, but you must pay both.)

Most of you will get paid *4000-5000 DM* per month for your "first" *Festvertrag* in an "A" or "B" house. As an *Anfänger* (beginner for your first two years in the German *fest* system, no matter how much experience you have.), the theaters may pay you as little as *3500DM* per month. We are not trying to discourage you here, but we are committed to you as fellow Americans, and are therefore sharing the "plain truth" about the German *Fest* Theater System.

✱✱✱

Actual Pay Schemes

All schemes are actual for July, 2000.

Gross monthly salary: 3,500.00DM

Deductions:

Lohnsteuer:	503.83
Kirchensteuer:	45.34
SolZ:	27.71
KV:	227.50
PV:	29.75
RV:	337.75
AV:	113.75 Total deductions: 1,285.63DM

Net Pay: **2,214.37DM**

Remember, we have to deduct an additional 8.5 percent for the BVK and agent fees:

3,500.00DM	monthly gross income
x 8.5%	
297.50DM	BVK & agent fees
2,214.37DM	previous net income
-297.50DM	BVK & agent fees
1,916.87DM	

True Net Pay: 1,916.87DM

Let us say this again; this is the present low-end salary range for beginners in Germany who are single with no dependents, paying an agent, and paying the church tax. Remember colleagues, these are German Marks, not U.S. dollars. As of March, 2000 the rate of exchange is 1USD= 2DM, the highest it has been in over 10 years! (Now the exchange rate is nearly to 2.20DM.)

Now, for more pay examples:

Gross monthly salary: **5,000.00DM**

Deductions:

Lohnsteuer:	990.25		
Kirchensteuer:	89.12		
SolZ:	54.46		
KV:	325.00		
PV:	42.50		
RV:	482.50		
AV:	162.50	Total deductions:	2,146.33DM
Net Pay:	**2,853.67DM**		

Don't forget to deduct an additional 8.5 percent for the BVK and agent fees:

5,000.00DM	monthly gross income
x 8.5%	
425.00DM	*BVK* & agent fees
2,853.67DM	previous net income
-425.00DM	*BVK* & agent fees
2,428.67DM	

True Net Pay: **2,428.67DM**

Gross monthly salary: **8,000.00DM** (a great salary)

Deductions:

Lohnsteuer: 2,176.75DM (See how much this increases?)

Kirchensteuer:	195.90DM	
SolZ:	119.72DM	
KV:	419.25DM	
PV:	54.83DM	
RV:	772.00DM	
AV:	260.00DM	Total deductions: 3,998.45DM

Net Pay: 4,001.55DM

Again, we have to deduct an additional 8.5 percent for the BVK and agent fees:

8,000DM	gross monthly income
x 8.5%	BVK & agent fees
680DM	

4,001.55DM	previous net pay
-680.00DM	BVK & agent fees
3,321.55DM	

True Net Pay: 3,321.55DM

Remember, the *Kirchensteuer* can be eliminated. And if you have dependents, that will change your tax basis considerably.

Try to keep all of this information in its proper perspective. We realize to many of you, that these numbers are shocking. However, let us put all of this in the proper context.

Seven years ago, in the house where I (William) am currently engaged, the baritone was paid 6,500-7,500DM per month. The rate of exchange was 1USD = 1.50DM. It doesn't take a mathematician to see the difference. In addition, back then, *Krankenversicherung* cost as much as 50 percent less, there was no *Solidaritätszuschlag* (this was added later to finance the rebuilding of the former East Germany), and *Lohnsteuer* was much less.

What has also drastically changed are the guesting possibilities. Eight years ago, if one was *fest*-engaged in an "A" house, he or she was practically guaranteed extra performances (at least five or 10, sometimes as many as 20) in other theaters. Even at only 3,000DM per performance, it's not hard to see the difference it would have made in one's income.

Consider the following:

1993 Season

7,000.00DM
x 60% (about the amount of deductions at that time)
4,200.00DM
x 13 months
54,600.00DM (annual net pay at that time)

3,000DM
x 10 guestings
30,000DM gross pay from guestings
x 50% (the extra income would put you in a higher tax bracket)
15,000DM   net pay from guestings

54,600DM
+15,000DM
69,600DM   net annual income
÷12
5,800DM   net monthly income

÷1.50   the rate of exchange at the time
$3,866.67(USD) net monthly income in U.S. Dollars

I don't know about you, but seven years ago, if I were a single person (or even married with children), I would have had no trouble living off a *$3,867 a month take-home pay.*

***

Today-2000

Now, compare that to our last example where a singer makes 8,000DM (gross income) a month, but with no guesting gigs, and with today's tax basis and rate of exchange:

8,000DM	monthly gross income
x 50%	deductions
4,000DM	monthly net income
x 13 months	
52,000DM	annual net income
52,000DM	
÷ 12	
*4,333DM_*	*average monthly income*
÷ 2	today's rate of exchange
$2,166.50-	**average net monthly income in U.S. Dollars**

There you have it. A single singer making 7,000DM per month with 10 guestings in 1993 brought home nearly twice as much as the same singer today making 8,000DM with no guestings. Even if you took away the guestings in the first example, the difference between what our singer earned then, and what he would earn now is still $1,000 (USD) per month. We are just trying to help you see how much the business here has changed. If you are going to Germany to get rich, go start an Internet company instead.

Do not let this hold you back from following your dreams!

Again, we are not trying to discourage you, but we want you to see the whole picture, should you decide to go into this profession.

***

Another way to increase your net pay

Never forget this: Just because your agent negotiated your first contract, you are not obligated to have him renegotiate it if you have been *verlängert* (kept for the following season) after your initial contract is up. If he has never been to one of your performances, nor sent you on any auditions during your first two years, it is our recommendation that you go straight to the boss, and tell him or her that you do not wish to involve the agent in your next contract. Ask the theater to add to your income what they were previously paying the agent. *That's equivalent to a 7 percent raise* (or more, because of the increase in net pay since you will no longer be paying an agent), and since the theater will not be paying out any more money than they previously were, they will be more than happy to do this. However, keep in mind that you will probably not ever work for that particular agent again. Ask yourself this: Does it really make sense to continue working with that particular agent if he hasn't done anything for you in two years? You will have to make that decision on your own.

A word about the *Bayrischer Versorgungskammer:* If you have worked more than 120 months, you may draw on the *BKV* fund (like an American 401K fund) in addition to regular German social security when you are 65. If you have not reached 120 months, and after two years of *not* working on the German stage, you may apply to get back all moneys *you* have contributed to the fund, *if* you agree *not* to work in the German theater system ever again. Remember, friends, "never" is a long time, so think this one over.

***

Pay for Non-Resident Guests

The previous pay schemes are only for those who are *fest* singers, and whose residence is Germany. What follows is an actual scheme taken this year (2000) from the pay statement of an American singer who was guesting in Germany. We will refer to the singer as Jane Doe.

Jane was paid *350DM per day* for the rehearsal period, which was spread out over three months. There was a guarantee of at least *35 rehearsal days* during that three-month period. She was paid *4,500DM per performance*, and guaranteed *eight performances* during a four month period. In addition, the theater agreed to pay her airfare. However, the theater considered the cost of the airline ticket *additional income to her*, as does the German *Finanzamt* (equivalent to our IRS), thereby greatly increasing her tax liability.

Imagine Jane's horror when she received her first pay statement from the theater. (She had already been in Germany for one month.) However, because of the nature of the work and a very erratic rehearsal schedule, she rehearsed only nine days during that first month. One might think, "OK, I've rehearsed nine days. At 350DM a day, that comes to 3,150DM for my first easy month of rehearsals. I can live off that. Right?" Think again.

Here are the actual deductions from Jane's pay statement:

Monies paid to the artist

Gross pay for nine days of rehearsal at 350DM per day:
3,150.00DM

Travel expenses (airline ticket):	3,087.39DM
Total "income":	6,237.39DM

Monies paid to other parties by the theater

BVK	(8% of 3,150.00DM)	252.00DM
Agent fee	(6% of 3,150.00DM)	189.00DM
Sales tax on agent fee (16%)		30.24DM

Taxes and other deductions

Income tax (30 percent, based on gross income plus *BVK*, theater's portion) 1,946.82DM

Solidarity tax (1.6 percent based on the same amount)		107.07DM
Agent fee	(6% of 3,150.00DM)	189.00DM
Sales tax on agent fee	(16% of 189.00DM)	30.24DM
Artist's contribution to *BVK*	(8% of 3,150.00DM)	252.00DM
Airline ticket		3,087.39DM
Total deductions:		5,612.52DM
Total pay:		6,237.39DM
Deductions:		-5,612.52DM

Total Net Pay:	***624.87DM***

Jane's net pay was actually $284.03 (USD) for her first month of rehearsal.

Obviously, it was the taxes on the airline ticket that took her to the cleaners during that first month. Her total net pay would have been 1,683.36DM (a whopping $765.16 USD) without the taxes on the ticket.

Jane's second and third months were considerably better since there were no travel expenses added to her income. Each month provided 13 days of rehearsal. The gross pay was 4,550DM. After all her deductions, the net pay was 2680.50DM ($1,218.41 USD)

For each performance, Jane received roughly the same net pay as each of the last two months of rehearsal.

These are actual figures. In no way were they altered or manipulated.

Lessons learned?

First, make your own travel arrangements. Then ask the theater to reimburse the cost of the expenses, plus enough to cover taxes you incur as a result of those reimbursements. Second, if you know you are going to be in the country for more than a month of rehearsal, *never* agree to a daily per diem. Insist on a weekly one, and make sure it is enough to live off. Third, make sure you know *in advance* exactly how much money you will receive in your hand at the end of the month. One does, after all, have to eat and pay the rent.

***

Remember, as a guest singer in Germany, you will expect the following deductions:

Lohnsteuer (Income tax)

30%

Solidaritätzuschlag (Solidarity tax for rebuilding eastern Germany)

1.6%

Bayrischer Versorgungskammer (Bavarian Retirement Fund)

8%

Note: The theater contributes an additional 8 percent to the fund, based on the gross income. The 8 percent is then added to the income, and this total amount (income +8%) becomes the taxable income.
Vermittlungsprovision (Agent fee) (when applicable)

10%

Umsatzsteuer (Sales tax on the agent fee)

16% *of the agent fee*

Bottom line:

Expect to net only 50 percent of your gross income as a guest. If the theater says they are paying *Reisekosten* (travel expenses), make it clear to them that you do not expect to pay taxes on those expenses, or at least ask them to make up for it in the form of extra pay.

A Word About Currency

As most readers should know by now, beginning January, 2002 there will no longer be a German Mark, Swiss Franc, or Austrian Shilling. The currency in the 13 participating European countries will be the Euro, designated as: € The rate of exchange between the existing currencies and the Euro has already been set. For example, one Euro is equal to 1.96 German Marks. As of April, 2001, the rate of exchange between the U.S. dollar and the German Mark is actually $1.00 = 2.20DM.

Therefore, $1.00 = € 1.13. We still emphasize using your credit card whenever possible. Nevertheless, as with all foreign currencies, be aware of the rate of exchange before you pull out your wallet.

Chapter Sixteen

Social Perks

Germany offers many social perks that can help you along. After all, where do you think all of that tax money is going? The following applies for those that are "*fest*" or at least a legal resident of Germany.

First, you pay nothing when you go to the doctor. Even having a child does not leave you with any hospital bills. The same goes for operations and emergencies.

The rules for *Kindergeld* (money given to you for raising your children) has changed almost every year over the course of the past five years. It is paid out by the theater or *Arbeitsamt*. Ask your theater's *Buchhaltung* (bookkeeping or payroll) for more details.

Erziehungsgeld (money for child rearing) is given to the mother of a newborn for the first 24 months of the child's life. She receives 600DM per month taxfree. This is paid out by the *Versorgungsamt*.

Wohngeld (subsidized housing) is paid out by the *Sozialamt*. It is paid to those whose rent exceeds a percentage of their income. It is calculated on the basis of dependents, income, utilities and the size of one's apartment.

Take advantage of all of these benefits. *You are paying for them.*

***

Do Your Taxes!

One of our favorite words is *Freibetrag* (tax exemption). Take as many as legally possible, just as you would in the States. When you receive your *Steuerkarte* (tax-classification card) from the *Einwohnermeldeamt* (resident registration office), make sure you are registered in the correct *Steuerklass* (tax bracket). If you are *ledig* (single), you are *Klass I* (one). If you are *verheiratet* (married), you are *Klass III* (three). They have also been changing the *Kinderfreibeträge* (child deductions). Therefore, always have your passport as well as your spouse's and children's in hand, if possible, when you pick-up your *Steuerkarte.* Then, if possible, go to a recommended *Steuerberater* (tax advisor). You will need him later anyway. Ask him/her to make sure that everything is *in Ordnung* (in order).

Chapter Seventeen

Arbeitslos
(Unemployed)

One of the least favorite words in this business is *gekündigt* (fired). Nevertheless, if you are here for any length of time, no matter what kind of singer you are, it will probably happen to you or someone you know. Usually, it will be because of a change of personnel at the theater, most likely the *Intendant*.

By law, the theater must inform their soloists by *October 15* whether they will be let go for the following season. If nothing is said to you *in writing* by that time, your contract is automatically extended for another season. If they do not let you go, but *you* want to leave, you must inform them in writing by *October 31*.

If they fire you and you do not find another job, and you have worked at least two seasons, you are eligible for *Arbeitslosengeld* (unemployment). Your unemployment is based on the average of your last three months' pay. It will be 60-65 percent of your *net* pay with a *maximum* allowance of about 2,800DM per month. The length of your draw is based on your length of employment. You must have a valid *Aufenthaltserlaubnis* to receive this. (This is where things get tricky.) "But my visa runs out on the last day of my employment," you say. Do not fret!

As an American, you have *Anspruch* (the right) to stay in Germany if you can sustain yourself and your dependents. They (the German government) must (as of this writing) extend your visa, even if it is only to receive *Arbeitslosengeld*. Of course, you have to meet the "length of employment" requirements. Do not let any *Beamter* (government employee) at the *Arbeitsamt* (employment office) try and hustle you into thinking otherwise. Stand up for your rights. In some of the offices in the former East Germany, there are still employees who are simply unaware of these things, even after ten years of the Wall being gone. Do not be rude, but courteous and stand your ground at the same time. You will eventually get your unemployment. Again, you have paid for it through your *Lohnsteuer* and 16 percent sales tax!

If for some reason you have been let go, make sure you go to the theater *Buchhaltung* (bookkeeping) personnel a couple of months before the season is over. This is very important, and you are pretty much at their mercy. (So be *very* nice to them.) Before you can receive any unemployment, they must fill out a stack of papers a mile high. Make sure this gets done *before* the season is over, so you can begin drawing on your unemployment right away. As the Germans say, *"Mann kann nicht nur von Luft und Liebe leben!"* ("One cannot live by air and love alone.")

Once you begin drawing unemployment, you are not as free as you think. You may not go *anywhere* without informing them first. Even if you are traveling only a couple of hours away to do an audition, you are still required to inform your assigned *Beamter* (government employee) at the *Arbeitsamt*. No, you may not hop on a plane and go to your mom's in Kalamazoo for a couple of weeks, and still draw your unemployment, unless you are using the two weeks of *Urlaub* (vacation) they give you each year. You may, however, unregister (*abmelden*) and go away for a period of time, and register (*anmelden*) again when you return, of course without pay.

The important thing to remember is this: As long as you receive unemployment, you are required to be reachable by the *Arbeitsamt at all times*, and unless otherwise given permission, physically be in the city of your residency. So make sure you are really clear on all of this.

Chapter Eighteen

Hard Learned Words of Wisdom

Okay, up until now, everything that you have read has been the "nuts and bolts" of auditioning and what to do once you land a position. The next few pages are just some of the peculiarities and other sundry things you may encounter and find confusing or troublesome once you are actually singing and working in Germany.

They include things like:

-Your relationship to your theater colleagues
-Getting a practice room or not being able to get one
-Rehearsal techniques
-The surprising freedom with which advertisers use the naked human form
-The European shopping experience

Your colleagues

Make an effort to learn the names of people with whom you are working at the theater. This includes your make-up person. There are many male make-up artists here as well as female, and they take pride in running the make-up and hair department of the theater. They work very, very hard for *you*. So do not forget, on opening night, if you are giving "*Toi, Toi, Toi!*" notes and cards to your colleagues, include them as well.

Also include your *Garderobe* (costume) person, your assistant stage director, and of course, the conductor. A *prima donna* or *primo uomo* attitude doesn't get you very far in the *fest* system. Even though many singers "think" the performance could not possibly be of the high caliber and professionalism and artistry it reaches without our grand singing (ha! ha!), we are way off-base not to remember all of the technicians, lighting designers, assistants, the *Souffleuse* (prompter), the stage director, the coaches, and all the others who gave of themselves to aid *you* in having an easy run with your singing that night. They matter, and you should *never* forget that.

A word about being double cast

Everyone is double-cast at one time or another, either *erste* (first) or *zweite Besetzung* (second cast). There is nothing more embarrassing than to have a guest or a new *fest* singer come to rehearsal with an attitude of resentment or contempt for their colleague because they are the *erste* or *zweite Besetzung*. We say embarrassing, because oftentimes the second cast finds themselves singing the première anyway because of sickness or extenuating circumstances. What a waste of energy to pitch a diva fit because you feel you have not had enough time with the orchestra or staging rehearsal, or for whatever reason. It also leaves you with a bad reputation. Don't think attitude will not catch up with you. It always does, sooner or later. Always be as professional as possible. If you have a problem with someone, talk to them. Do not do it in the presence of others. Ask the individual to join you for a coke in the canteen, or if you could meet with them at their studio to discuss something. Please, never disagree with your stage director, conductor, or other singing partner(s) in front of others at a rehearsal. This can be a quick career suicide move.

***

Krankgeschrieben (written sick)

Though this is definitely a perk of the German social system, we have intentionally chosen to place it in the "Words of Wisdom" chapter. You should exercise wisdom when utilizing this privilege. First, the buck stops with the doctor, and not with your employer. When your doctor says that you are *krankgeschrieben* (written sick), it is basically a permission slip to "stay out of school" for the day, or for however long he says. Having said this, there are some things you should consider.

If you come to rehearsal, you are expected to be healthy enough to sing, though you should certainly "mark" when necessary. We will talk about that next. If you are not healthy enough to sing, *stay home,* even if you want to come to rehearsal "just to watch." Besides, it is *very unprofessional* to come to a rehearsal sick. It is also not at all appreciated by your colleagues, who are doing everything they can do to stay healthy during the flu season that always seems to coincide with the opera season.

The first day you think you are getting sick, simply telephone the *KBB* and say, "I'm sick." That is your judgment call to make. However, if you are ill for more than one day, a *Krankenschein* (sickslip) is required from your doctor. Early on, establish a good relationship with an *HNO* or *Hals, Nase und Ohre* (ENT, or ear, nose, and throat) doctor who is sensitive to the needs of singers. Always ask the *KBB*. All theaters have a specific doctor whom they recommend. *Take advantage of this system, but do not abuse it.* We are proud to report, that Americans, because of their driven work ethic, have the reputation of abusing this system *the least*. There are, of course, exceptions. Unfortunately, when the system is abused, we all ultimately suffer, and people begin to think, "Singers are such babies!"–especially the non-singers who are responsible for hiring and firing you. So keep that in mind. *Again, use it, but do not abuse it.*

***

Singing Smart

Have you heard it said, "If you are going to Germany to sing, you are going to ruin your voice!"? The fact is, the opportunity is certainly there to be taken advantage of vocally. It is our opinion, that by your second season, you should try to secure a contract in which you sing not more than 40 performances per year. Obviously, in theaters with smaller ensembles, that is not always possible, unless you are the house diva or primo tenor. Nevertheless, at least try. Reducing the number of annual performances is only the beginning of protecting your voice while working in the *fest* system.

***

Markieren (marking)

Most singers should know what 'marking' means. It is singing with less than your full-voice, or as some say, "singing half-voice". Don't feel as though you have to sing full voice during every staging rehearsal, especially if you are doing several productions in one season. *Mark!* Of course every individual must find his or her own limit. Some singers actually prefer to sing full-out during much of the rehearsal period, especially when struggling with a new role, or even singing something in a completely different *Fach*. Another situation in which you may want to sing out, is if you are new in a theater, or a guest, and neither the stage director nor the conductor has heard you sing.

Try to keep this in mind: In Germany one usually rehearses for four to eight weeks compared to the usual two to four weeks in America.

Singers in Germany have to search for that fine line between marking too much and singing full voice. This is something you alone will have to judge for yourself. Please be wise: You have only one voice.

Orchestra Rehearsals

The same rules pertaining to marking while staging a production generally apply during the final two weeks of orchestra rehearsals as well. Most theaters will have one or two *Orchestersitzprobes* (rehearsal with the orchestra without staging, either in a rehearsal room or on the stage), as many as four to six *Bühnen- und Orchesterprobes* (on the stage, with the orchestra in the pit, and the singers doing minimal, if any staging), a *Klavierhauptprobe* (piano dress), an *Orchesterhauptprobe* (a somewhat relaxed orchestra dress rehearsal, where the director and/or conductor will occasionally stop), and the *Generalprobe* (the final orchestra dress). Whew!

We hope it is obvious to you, that if you are single cast as Leonora or Di Luna in Verdi's *Il Trovatore*, you are *not* going to sing full voice at every rehearsal, or you will have *no* voice for the première. This is compounded by the fact that at least half of these rehearsals (sometimes including the *Generalprobe* as well) will begin as early as 10.00. It is not uncommon to have an *Orchesterhauptprobe* on Wednesday evening from 18.00 until 22.00 or 23.00, the *Generalprobe* at 10.00 the next morning (often open to the public and where the press may be taping and/or filming) *and* the première on Friday evening. Don't assume you will always have a "black" night before the première. Just be pleasantly surprised when you do. Do you think you will hear the tenor sing "*Di Quella Pira....*" in full voice before opening night? Probably not, if he is single cast.

Something more to consider

By now you should already know this as a singer, but here it is any-way: The more prepared you are musically before you come to *any* rehearsal, the better you will sing; and the better you sing, the less likely it will be that you tire quickly at rehearsals. So, *be prepared*. Remember, it is *your* voice. No one else can protect it but you.

***

Practice Rooms

We all know how valuable a good practice room can be, especially if you have lived in New York City. Nothing is worse than having an audi-tion and not having any place to warm-up. Believe it or not, in many major cites (Düsseldorf, for example), you can go to the main library and rent a practice room for a nominal fee (5-10DM per hour). Also, try the churches. Even if you don't have an audition in a particular city, if you are lucky and extremely nice, you may sweet-talk the *Pförtner* at the theater into letting you use one of the practice rooms there during the day when no one is rehearsing. Unfortunately, practice rooms sim-ply do not exist for the agent auditions. It is still a mystery to all who have auditioned for them as to why. So, you will have to take advantage of a phone booth on the corner, the agent's bathroom, or even the bath-room on the train.

***

European "Openness"

"Nudity, etc." What an attention-grabbing line, not to mention a rather effective advertising device. Expect to see a lot of it while on the continent. Nudity in Europe is a rather blasé and well-accepted part of life. It is all over the place; on television, on billboards, magazine covers (their version of TV Guide included), and yes, even in normal good ol' everyday life. There is a term in Germany, *FKK* or *Frei Körper Kultur* (free body culture), which is a tolerated freedom in which folks simply take *everything* off and sunbathe by the local stream, or soak up some sunshine in the buff. So if you see a sign that says "*FKK*," you know what to expect. Saunas are also a source of some consternation for Americans, for you are looked at rather oddly, should you sit in the steambath or sauna wrapped up in a terry-cloth towel. (Yes, those snickers and giggles you hear trailing after your exit are meant for you.)

Now, on the flip side of this coin, you can feel quite safe and secure if you are out walking late in the evening. Streets are well patrolled by police, and violent crimes are a much less common occurrence in Germany than in the U.S. So if you have a late train, do not worry if you have a five-to-10 minute walk home. You will get there safely. The weirdest thing you may encounter are the beggars in the larger towns and the open drunkenness that is alive and thriving. Public drinking or drunkenness is not against the law. As you would in New York, keep your eyes directed forward, look as though you know where you are going, and before you know it, the individual who was begging you for a Mark will be long gone.

***

The European Shopping Experience

Since we Americans are such a consumer-oriented society, the foremost question on everyone's mind would be the shopping situation. When we think back on our first weeks auditioning in Germany, we are stunned in some ways that we even made it through, much less landed a job. Here it is, nine years later, and we are just now realizing that no matter how hard we wish it were true, we will not be able to do our grocery shopping on a Sunday. (Unless of course, you consider hitting the *Drogerie* (equivalent to a 7-Eleven store) at the train station. Yes, the stores in the train stations are adequately stocked, but they are very expensive. So if you are watching your pennies, you should avoid such places that will only gouge your pocket book. At any rate, this section is to let you know about some of the oddities and little known secrets about being in Germany that you otherwise would have had to spend years figuring out.

***

Shopping Bags

Just as the American Express commercial says, "Don't leave home without it," we also advise, "Don't leave home without your shopping bag." One area where the Europeans certainly have us beat is their practice of *Umweltfreundlichkeits* (environmental friendliness). Just like your calling-card and passport, always have a plastic or cloth shopping bag tucked away in your backpack or purse. If not, expect to pay 30 *Pfennige* for plastic or 1-2DM for a cloth shopping bag. It makes sense if you think about it. This way there will not be millions of plastic bags lying in a landfill for thousands of years as there will be in the States.

***

Where to Get What

Stores fall into categories just a little bit differently in Germany than in the U.S. For example, if you wanted to buy some aspirin in America, you would run out to the drugstore, right? Well, strangely enough, there is a store here called *Drospa*, and to the naked eye it looks like a drug store. It carries things like suntan lotion, makeup, candy, baby accessories, film for your cameras, some vitamins, etc. You can even get blank cassette tapes there. However, try finding the aspirin, and you will be wasting your time. You can buy aspirin only at an *Apotheke*. Of course, you can buy tooth-care products and some makeup and even baby stuff at a *Drospa*, but be careful in assuming that just because a store looks as though it should have something in it, that it will.

Cigarettes? Yes, unfortunately, in every place, everywhere, anytime of day or night one can purchase cigarettes. But why would you want them as a singer anyway? (We'll touch on this subject later.) However, other necessities can take some effort. Most large cities, and even the not-so-large cities have a bi-weekly *Markt* (open-air market). This is an open-air farmer's market, where you can pick up the best, freshest, and most delicious fruits, veggies, eggs, meats, cheeses, breads, etc. They are usually held every Wednesday and Saturday at the town square from 7 a.m. until 2-4 p.m. Check them out. They are really worthwhile. Office supplies can be purchased at the larger department stores and specialty office supply stores. Those look just like ours do in the U.S. There are copy places here as well (like our Kinko's). Europe is just on another continent, not another planet.

***

Medicine

I'd like to spend a little more time on the *Apotheke*, the "real" drugstore. This is where you will be getting all of your medications, herbal mixtures, vitamins (although you can get those in other convenience stores such as *Drospa*, *Drogeriemarkt*, *Schlecker*, etc.) *Apothekes* are great. The staffs are very helpful, and they will usually try very hard to find out the medication you need, should it be something you normally buy in America. They simply go to their computers, look up your prescription, and more often than not, they are able to come up with a European equivalent. In addition to this convenience, every city has a 24-hour *Apotheke* service. In the window of each *Apotheke* there is a posted schedule which informs you of the "on-duty" pharmacy for any given day, in addition to that assigned pharmacy's telephone number. This includes holidays and Sundays.

***

Smoking in Europe

Everyone seems to do it! I don't know of anything that affected us more upon arriving in Europe as singers than the number of people who smoke. We are talking about other singers at auditions, the pianists, the technical staff at the theaters, patrons in restaurants, in the lobby at your bank, on the trains and S-bahns – *everywhere.* It was as though you were being thrust back into an era which most of us in the United States had left 'way behind. In fact, most of the people our age in America are not old enough to even remember that era. *The main point is this*: People still smoke in Europe, and heartily. This is their culture, and no matter how much you want to feign indignation and curse the lot of them, you may wind-up slitting your own throat. The best way to handle this is to just tell folks that you are highly allergic, or cannot stay long, be it a reception after your premiere, in the canteen at your theater, or at a dinner party, when people start to relax and take out their smokes. In addition, when boarding a train or looking for a table in a restaurant, always look for the words *Rauchen Verboten* (No Smoking!). Unfortunately, R.J. Reynolds still has a stronghold in Europe, and you will just have to deal with it.

***

E-Mailing from Germany

You can take along your laptop if you want, but don't expect to find a place to go on-line with it unless you have some *very* generous friends. Even making a local call costs, and can really add up. However, don't fret. There are cyber cafés popping up like mushrooms everyday.

Whenever you arrive in a city, simply ask around. A good place to begin would be the library or university. If you know in advance where you are going to be staying, try to locate the website(s) of that particular city. Most of them are multilingual. The *Karstadt* (a chain of department stores) also has Internet cafés at many of their locations.

***

Important Websites

We cannot imagine even one of you without an e-mail address, or at least having some knowledge of the Internet. Face it, the electronic age really is here to stay. So we might as well use it to our advantage. We know this will sound too simple, but this is it: *www.miz.org*. We mean it. If it has to do with music in Germany, and everything pertaining to it, this is *the* Web site. It will link you to everything. This includes all the *Musik Hochschule*, competitions, opera studios, and even most of the opera theaters, at least as of this writing. In addition there is another site, *www.theaterjob.de*, that promises to be a great website in the near future.

Also, go to *www.yahoo.de*, as we mentioned earlier, to search for more localized information throughout Germany.

***

Important telephone numbers

The American Embassy in Berlin-(030) 238 5174

Police/Emergency-110

Fire Station/Ambulance-112

Information (Telephone numbers)-Domestic-11833
-Foreign-11834

Bibliography

Auditioning in the 21st Century is a useful handbook for singers considering pursuing a career in the German-speaking countries of Europe. The book is a compilation of experiences, anecdotes and hard-learned lessons of the authors and other contributors. Information is presented in a relaxed and simple manner, including tips about helpful Websites to how voice-types are being categorized in today's market. This handbook is a necessity for any artist who is brave enough to embrace the challenges presented in pursuing a career abroad. Good reading, and good luck!

About the Authors

Soprano, Nada Radakovich began her formal musical training at the renowned Interlochen School of the Performing Arts. There she majored in cello, piano, and voice. She received both her Bachelor and Master of Music degrees in voice performance and opera from The University of Michigan School of Music. Presently Ms. Radakovich performs in the United States as well as in Europe, where she resides.

Born and raised in Atlanta, Georgia, baritone William Killmeier began his studies at The University of Georgia. He received his Bachelor of Music from Westminster Choir College in Princeton, New Jersey. As a member of the world renowned Westminster Choir, Mr. Killmeier frequently sang with the New York Philharmonic, the Philadelphia Orchestra, and at the Spoleto Festival. After graduation, he enlisted in the U.S. Army as soloist with The United States Army Band (Pershing's Own) and The U.S. Army Chorus. Following his enlistment in the military, Mr. Killmeier began his 'fest' career in Germany where he continues to perform after nearly ten years.

Index

Printed in the United States
50576LVS00003B/120

9 780595 186686